CW00369992

NETWORK TWO

An English course-book for secondary schools

KEITH HURST
Head of English
Robert May's School, Odiham

JOHN SIMES
Head of English
Houndsdown School, Totton

HODDER AND STOUGHTON
LONDON SYDNEY AUCKLAND TORONTO

PERSONAL ACKNOWLEDGEMENTS

We would like to thank Jean Hurst, Derek Fulford and Martin Willing from the many who gave us much valuable help and advice.

British Library Cataloguing in Publication Data

Hurst, Keith
  Network two.
  1. English language – Grammar – 1950–
  I. Title   II. Simes, John
  428   PE1128

  ISBN 0 340 25769 5

First published 1981

Copyright © 1981 K Hurst and J Simes

All rights reserved. No part of this publication may be reproduced or transmitted in any form or by any means, electronic or mechanical, including photocopying, recording, or any information storage and retrieval system, without permission in writing from the publisher.

Printed and bound in Great Britain for Hodder and Stoughton Educational, a division of Hodder and Stoughton Ltd, Mill Road Dunton Green, Sevenoaks, Kent,
by Richard Clay (The Chaucer Press) Ltd, Bungay, Suffolk
Typeset by Northumberland Press Ltd, Gateshead, Tyne and Wear

Contents

To the Teacher

The primary aim of this book is to provide literary and pictorial material, together with suggestions for work, designed to enable students to use language proficiently and purposefully.

We believe that it is not enough just to get students to speak and write, nor is it enough to get them to speak and write correctly. Free, expressive and personal writing and speaking which arise out of the experiences and interests of pupils and teacher are vitally important elements in helping young people to come to terms with themselves, each other and the world around them. However, as the Bullock Report observes:

> 'Children reach a point where they need new techniques, having run through the satisfaction of their spontaneous performances.'★

We offer this book to provide guidance at the point when this stage of development has been reached.

The material, here, has been chosen in the hope that it is both interesting and stimulating in its own right, but the stimuli should also be thought of as exempla – they are used to indicate some of the techniques employed in the everyday use of language. From them, we wish to develop rather more adaptable and varied language skills in children and young adults by making more varied demands upon them. Ideally, they should be able to operate in a number of different language contexts; this book is organised in such a way as to identify these contexts and to suggest structured activities in reading, talking, listening and writing.

The exercises are arranged to offer a sense of progression but we do not believe that this makes flexibility impossible. Together with the passages and illustrations, they may well provoke discussion on moral, social and aesthetic subjects, not just those of purely linguistic interest. Most can easily be linked with thematic studies (an index is provided with this in mind) or the study of literature. Just as importantly, some are designed to appeal to pupils of low ability, others

★A LANGUAGE FOR LIFE H.M.S.O. 1975

to the very able, and many can satisfactorily be attempted by a wide ability range.

Much of the later material may provide useful induction for students wishing to work towards an advanced course in English literature.

Throughout the book, we employ a method of direct address to the student. This is in no way intended to provide a substitute for the intimate involvement of the classroom teacher.

The teacher may well rework much of the rubric according to the needs of, and his or her relationship with, the students. We hope that much of the material and the general line of approach will trigger a good many of the teacher's own ideas and, whilst NETWORK **can** constitute a course of study, we suggest it might also be employed as a reference manual.

DESCRIPTION

Cutting your cloth

It is to be hoped that much of your descriptive writing will be taken on for the sheer pleasure of becoming an artist with words. But always remember that descriptions have many functions and can be written with a variety of aims in mind. The following exercises might underline this point.

D1 Imagine that you want to describe a horse to a young child who has not yet seen one. You will need to build a detailed, accurate and vivid description so that at a later date, the child will be able to recognise such a creature from your description. Write the description down.

D2 Compare your description with those which follow:

a) *Huge in the dense grey – ten together –*
   Megalith still. They breathed, making no move,
   With draped manes and tilted hind-hooves,
   Making no sound
   I passed: not one snorted or jerked its head.
   Grey silent fragments
   Of a grey silent world.

b) Quadruped. Graminivorous. Forty teeth, namely, twenty-four grinders, four eye-teeth, and twelve incisive. Sheds coat in the spring; in marshy countries, sheds hoofs, too. Hoofs hard, but requiring to be shod with iron. Age known by marks in mouth.

c) He has won nine races over hurdles, and was particularly impressive at Haydock Park recently when, carrying 12st 12lb, he came up from behind to win the Embassy Handicap Hurdle by seven lengths, conceding the runner-up 33 lbs. He acts well on soft ground, and gives the impression of being a genuine stayer, even though he is comparatively inexperienced, and no horse of his age has yet won this highly competitive event.

d) Silhouetted against the black sky, the silver stallion reared and pawed the air, letting out a shrill, defiant scream. As he lowered his striking hoofs his mane rose and fell in a myriad of silver. Again he rose and challenged the night, towering into the vast emptiness around, a seething mass of hoofs and bared teeth, half fury and half triumph.

e) Solid hoofed quadruped with flowing mane and tail, used as beast of burden and draught and for riding on.

Every one of these was written by a different person for a different reason.

Compare the styles of each description.
Where do you think the descriptions come from?

Try describing a person you know in three different ways for three different purposes. Here are some possible purposes which you can choose from:
a) job reference
b) teacher's report
c) a 'missing persons' file
d) as though you yourself are the person – describing yourself in a letter to a penfriend.

People

Study the following descriptions of people and discuss the details which each author has chosen to include.

MAMMON

Like a melted slab of marble he lay face down, sprawled out on an airbed beside his private swimming pool. A bikini'd girl sat massaging his shoulders while he groaned with pleasure. Transluscent rolls of flab spilled over the top of his elasticated Bermuda shorts. A daisied flip-flop swung from the stubby toe of his raised foot and he dabbled a large pudding-like hand in the cool water of the pool. This luminously pale body gleamed, clammy and glutinous in the heat.

Aware of my approach he rolled over and casually glanced up. His watery eyes still fixed on me, he stretched out, took hold of a large box of chocolates, offered me one which I refused and proceeded to dip into it, retrieving the delicacies and popping them excitedly into his large shapeless mouth. He then sucked each sticky finger with great precision, his thick salivary lips greedily consuming all traces of the chocolate.

'The very best' he mumbled incoherently, and I assumed he was referring to the bulging contents of his mouth. 'I only ever get the very best', he continued, snapping his fingers to which the bikini'd girl automatically picked up a cigar packet, took out a cigar and placed it between his lips. 'Why bother to live if you don't intend to get the best out of life?' The unlit cigar stuck to his lower lip as he spoke. He leant forward as the girl held a flashy silver lighter to his mouth. He inhaled, tilted his head back and pouting his lips blew out the smoke slowly, watching it coil and disappear. 'Only fools endure discomfort. My motto is keep number one happy' he pointed emphatically to himself, 'and everything'll be fine.'

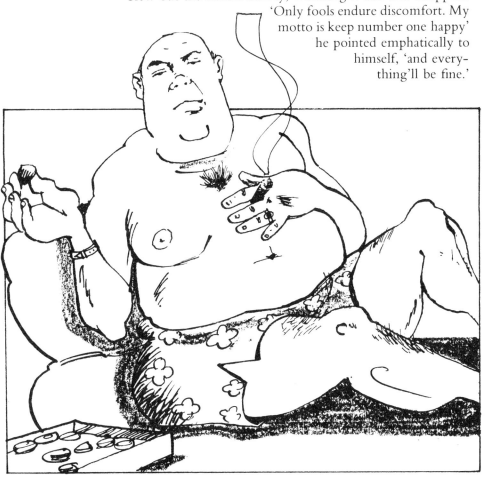

He then snapped his fingers again and pointed to his empty
glass which was instantly refilled. Sipping the cocktail drink
he lay back. His stomach like a rising lump of dough inflated
as he noisily breathed in and out. He licked the dribbles from
around his mouth.

'Just give me plenty of the best', he concluded, and sighed
as the girl continued to pummel his left shoulder-blade.

by Louise Gower (aged seventeen)

'Now, what I want is, Facts. Teach these boys and girls
nothing but Facts. Facts alone are wanted in life. Plant
nothing else, and root out everything else. You can only form
the minds of reasoning animals upon Facts: nothing else will
ever be of any service to them. This is the principle on which
I bring up my own children, and this is the principle on which
I bring up these children. Stick to Facts, sir!'

The scene was a plain, bare, monotonous vault of a school-room, and the speaker's square forefinger emphasised his observations by underscoring every sentence with a line on the schoolmaster's sleeve. The emphasis was helped by the speaker's square wall of a forehead, which had his eyebrows for its base, while his eyes found commodious cellarage in two dark caves, overshadowed by the wall ... The emphasis was helped by the speaker's voice, which was inflexible, dry, and dictatorial. The emphasis was helped by the speaker's hair, which bristled on the skirts of his bald head, a plantation of firs to keep the wind from its shining surface, all covered with knobs, like the crust of a plum pie, as if the head had scarcely warehouse-room for the hard facts stored inside. The speaker's obstinate carriage, square coat, square legs, square shoulders – nay, his very neckcloth, trained to take him by the throat with an unaccommodating grasp, like a stubborn fact, as it was – all helped the emphasis.

'In this life, we want nothing but Facts, sir; nothing but Facts!'

The speaker, and the schoolmaster, and the third grown person present, all backed a little and swept with their eyes the inclined plane of little vessels then and there arranged in order, ready to have imperial gallons of facts poured into them until they were full to the brim.

from HARD TIMES by Charles Dickens

Can you guess anything about these people which the writers don't tell us? How?
Notice the details used, the words, the metaphors and similes.

To say as much as possible about a person, it is often necessary to write about more than the person's face. What other noticeable details give us an idea of a person's character?

D5

With a partner or group, think of someone you all know and discuss all the significant details about them that you can think of.
List these on paper.

D6

Can you classify these details? Do they come under headings like Clothing, Habits etc? Consider a list of possible headings and see how some of the details chosen for this passage compare with yours.

Mr Farr trod delicately and disgustedly down the dark, narrow stairs like a man on ice. He knew, without looking or slipping, that vicious boys had littered the darkest corners with banana peel; and when he reached the lavatory, the basins would be choked and the chains snapped on purpose. He remembers 'Mr Farr, no father' scrawled in brown, and the day the sink was full of blood that nobody admitted having lost. A girl rushed past him up the stairs, knocked the papers out of his hand, did not apologize, and the loose meg of his cigarette burned his lower lip as he failed to open the lavatory door. I heard from inside his protest and rattlings, the sing-song whine of his voice, the stamping of his small patent-leather shoes, his favourite swear-words – he swore, violently and privately, like a collier used to thinking in the dark – and I let him in.

'Do you always lock the door?' he asked, scurrying to the tiled wall.

'It stuck,' I said.

He shivered, and buttoned.

He was the senior reporter, a great shorthand writer – a chain-smoker, a bitter drinker, very humorous, round-faced and round-bellied, with dart holes in his nose. Once, I thought as I stared at him then in the lavatory of the offices of the Tawe News, he might have been a mincing-mannered man, with a strut and a cane to balance it, a watch-chain across the waistcoat, a gold tooth, even, perhaps a flower from his own garden in his buttonhole. And now each attempt at a precise gesture was caked and soaked before it began; when he placed the tips of his thumb and forefinger together, you saw only the cracked nails in mourning and Woodbine stains. He gave me a cigarette and shook his coat to hear matches.

from A PORTRAIT OF THE ARTIST AS A YOUNG DOG
by Dylan Thomas

You can often tell a great deal about an individual from the way in which he speaks. Language, dialect, accent and his choice of words can often say as much about a character as a facial expression.

Speech can help to give an immediate and vivid impression of a character:

Another friend of that period was six-foot Billy, who ate regularly in the cafe downstairs – a stranded Negro sailor from Troy, Missouri, who had either jumped ship or had lost his way. I never knew where he slept, or how he lived, but every evening he'd be there in his pew, dropping great lumps of butter into his hot strong tea and carefully stripping the bones from a kipper. His huge fat cheeks were lightly scarred by knives, and the marks of knuckle-dusters ran across his eyebrows. But he was sleepily gentle, never raised his voice, and his favourite diversions seemed to be tea and gossip. Billy was an excellent listener, and it seemed impossible to bore him. He'd salute the dullest story with the most flattering attention. 'Waal, ah'll go slash mah wrists, if that ain't sumpin',' he'd murmur. 'You may hang me up by mah entrails.' Sometimes he'd disappear for a few days, then pop up, beaming. 'Gouge mah eyes, shuh good to see you.'

from AS I WALKED OUT ONE MIDSUMMER MORNING
by Laurie Lee

Can you build up character descriptions from these photographs (below and on page 12)?

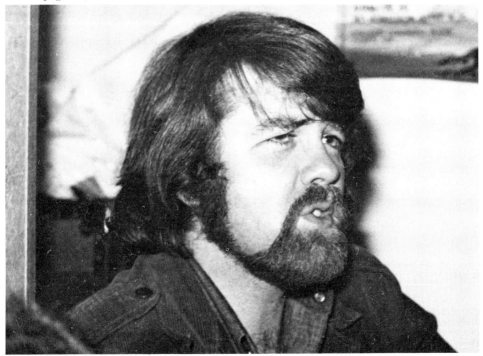

Scenes

Artists often practise their skills by painting scenes of perfectly motionless objects. Such a picture is called a 'still life'. All pictures are still, of course, but most (apart from these) capture a moment in which movement is suggested but suspended.

Try writing your own 'still life', either by using the photograph on the cover or a collection of objects in front of you.

Writers can sometimes capture a moment rather like a painter does; a moment of suspended time. Read these examples of **almost** still life and then see if you can describe a similar occasion. For example, the tension and dead silence before the start of a race.

> The pigs lay, bloated bags of fat, sensuously enjoying the shadows under the trees. There was no wind and they were unsuspicious; and practice had made Jack silent as the shadows. He stole away again and instructed his hidden hunters. Presently they all began to inch forward, sweating in the silence and heat. Under the trees an ear flapped idly. A little apart from the rest, sunk in deep maternal bliss, lay the largest sow of the lot. She was black and pink; and the great bladder of her belly was fringed with a row of piglets that slept or burrowed and squeaked.
>
> Fifteen yards from the drove Jack stopped; and his arm, straightening, pointed at the sow. He looked round in inquiry to make sure that everyone understood and the other boys nodded at him. The row of right arms slid back. 'Now!'

from LORD OF THE FLIES by William Golding

> Not a human being was out of doors at the dairy. The denizens were all enjoying the usual afternoon nap of an hour or so which the exceedingly early hours kept in summertime rendered a necessity. At the door the wood-hooped pails, sodden and bleached by infinite scrubbings, hung like hats on a stand upon the forked and peeled limb of an oak fixed there for that purpose; all of them ready and dry for the evening milking. Angel entered, and went through the silent passages of the house to the back quarters, where he

listened for a moment. Sustained snores came from the cart-house, where some of the men were lying down; the grunt and squeal of sweltering pigs arose from the still further distance. The large-leaved rhubarb and cabbage plants slept too, their broad limp surfaces hanging in the sun like half-closed umbrellas.

from TESS OF THE D'URBERVILLES by Thomas Hardy

D10

Now is the time to see whether it is easier or more difficult to do what a painter cannot do – paint a picture in which a great deal of activity takes place and show how it develops. Remembering the need for significant detail, describe:

- a) a crowded city street
- b) a sweltering seaside resort
- c) a fair
- d) a street market
- e) the school corridors at breaktime.

Try to make the reader feel as though he is there by describing sounds, sights, smells and sensations. Every busy scene consists of small incidents, some of which must be picked out and described as they force themselves on a watcher's attention in real life. You may find that some of the techniques used in this poem are of help to you:

BELSHAZZAR

> *That day in the city there were banners slung*
> *Across the streets, from balconies and chimneys,*
> *Swinging in the wind like smoke, and telegraph poles*
> *Were hung with geraniums; military bands*
> *Marched down the thoroughfares and bugles rang*
> *Against the plate-glass frontages. And in that night*
> *There were fireworks in the public parks at twilight,*
> *Laburnums of flame that flowered and fell through the air,*
> *And high on the hill the palace windows blazed*
> *Like the shell of a house on fire. And in that night*
> *The uniforms moved along the lobbies, gold and scarlet,*
> *Gold and blue, and shoulders were sugared with jewels*
> *Under the hanging icicles of chandeliers.*
> *They poured the yellow wine in the grey silver,*
> *The red in the yellow gold, and plates were piled*
> *With quails and nightingales and passion fruit,*

And the air was a fume of music. And in that night
The King sat above his court, speaking to none,
Small and grotesque there in a high-backed chair,
His hands gripping the carved griffins, his eyes
Like halves of hard-boiled eggs. He stared at the wall,
At the bare plaster above the footmen's heads.
The music and laughter ceased, the people were silent,
They put down their forks and raised no cup to the mouth,
But turned and stared at the wall where the King was staring.
And there was nothing on the wall at all.

Norman Nicholson

Compare your efforts with the following passages:

A stout man with a pink face wears dingy white flannel trousers, a blue coat with a pink handkerchief showing, and a straw hat much too small for him, perched at the back of his head. He plays the guitar. A little chap in white canvas shoes, his face hidden under a felt hat like a broken wing, breathes into a flute; and a tall thin fellow, with bursting over-ripe button boots, draws ribbons – long, twisted, streaming ribbons – of tune out of a fiddle. They stand, unsmiling, but not serious, in the broad sunlight opposite the fruit-shop; the pink spider of a hand beats the guitar, the little squat hand, with a brass-and-turquoise ring, forces the reluctant flute, and the fiddler's arm tries to saw the fiddle in two.

A crowd collects, eating oranges and bananas, tearing off the skins, dividing, sharing. One young girl has even a basket of strawberries, but she does not eat them. 'Aren't they **dear**!' She stares at the tiny pointed fruits as if she were afraid of them. The Australian soldier laughs. 'Here, go on, there's not more than a mouthful.' But he doesn't want her to eat them, either. He likes to watch her little frightened face, and her puzzled eyes lifted to his. 'Aren't they a **price**!' He pushes out his chest and grins. Old fat women in velvet bodices – old dusty pin-cushions – lean old hags like worn umbrellas with a quivering bonnet on top; young women, in muslins, with hats that might have grown on hedges, and high pointed shoes; men in khaki, sailors, shabby clerks, young Jews in fine cloth suits with padded shoulders and wide trousers, 'hospital boys' in blue – the sun discovers them – the loud, bold music holds them together in one big knot for a moment. The young ones are larking, pushing each other on and off the pavement, dodging, nudging; the old ones are

talking: 'So I said to 'im, if you wants the doctor to yourself, fetch 'im, says I.'

'An' by the time they was cooked there wasn't so much
as you could put in the palm of me 'and!'

The only ones who are quiet are the ragged children. They
stand, as close up to the musicians as they can get, their hands
behind their backs, their eyes big. Occasionally a leg hops,
an arm wags. A tiny staggerer, overcome, turns around
twice, sits down solemn, and then gets up again.

from BANK HOLIDAY by Katherine Mansfield

Stepping in from the torrid street, you met a band of
cool air like fruit-peel pressed to your brow, and entered
a cloistered grotto laden with the tang of shellfish, wet tiles,
and wine-soaked wood. There was no waiting, no crowding;
the place was yours; pot-boys took your orders with ringing cries; and men stood at their ease holding goblets of
sherry, with plenty of time to drink them, while piled round
the counters – succulently arranged in dishes or enthroned
on great blocks of ice – lay banquets of sea-food; craggy
oysters, crabs, calamares heaped in golden rings, fresh
lobsters twitching on beds of palm-leaves, bowls of mussels,
and feathery shrimps. Also on offer would be the little
sizzling saucers of kidney or roasted sparrow, snails, fried
squid, hot prawns in garlic, stewed pork or belly of lamb.
Nobody drank without eating – it would have been thought
uncivilized (and may have been one of the reasons why no
one was drunk). But then this sea-food, after all, was some
of the best in the world, land-locked Madrid's particular
miracle, freshly gathered that morning from the far-away
shores – the Mediterranean, Biscay, Atlantic – and rushed
to the capital in special trains which pushed everything else
into the sidings.

That's how I remember it: under the terra-cotta roofs,
a proliferation of caves of ice. With carters, porters, watch-
men, taxi-drivers, sleek dandies, and plump officials sipping
their golden wines, fastidiously peeling a prawn, biting into
the tart pink flesh of a lobster, tasting the living brine of
half-forgotten seas, of half-remembered empires, while the
surge of conversation continued like bubbling water under
the framed pictures of bulls and heroes. It was a way of
life evolved like a honeycomb and buried away from the
burning sky; and perhaps no other city at that time had so

successfully come to terms with the particular priority of pleasure.

from AS I WALKED OUT ONE MIDSUMMER MORNING
by Laurie Lee

D12 It is often necessary to give some definite shape to events taking place in a scene. Your description may be building up to some important moment, as in the 'sleeping pigs' passage above, or here, where a number of events are taking place in the same split second:

Voices were starting, but no one focused on them. They were snapped short from the rear of the room. A wind seemed to whip Shane's shirt at the shoulder and the glass of the front window beyond shattered near the bottom.

Then I saw it.

It was mine alone. The others were turning to stare at the back of the room. My eyes were fixed on Shane and I saw it. I saw the whole man move, all of him, in the single  flashing instant. I saw the head lead and the body swing and the driving power of the legs beneath. I saw the arm leap and the hand take the gun in the lightning sweep. I saw the barrel line up like – like a finger pointing – and the flame spurt even as the man himself was still in motion.

And there on the balcony Fletcher, impaled in the act
of aiming for a second shot, rocked on his heels and fell
back into the open doorway behind him. He clawed at the
jambs and pulled himself forward. He staggered to the rail
and tried to raise the gun. But the strength was draining
out of him and he collapsed over the rail, jarring it loose
and falling with it.

from SHANE by Jack Schaefer

D13   Describe the events leading up to an accident, or the crowds
in the street waiting for the arrival of some very important
person. Build your scene up to a moment of drama.

*Something is about to happen. Describe the moment of poise and the
event which follows.*

NARRATIVE

In considering how to write a story, it is worth looking at it with three sets of people in mind:

a) the characters in the story
b) the writer
c) the reader.

What relationship should exist between these people? Here are some possibilities:

i) Is the writer one of the characters in the story? Or the **only** character?
ii) Is the writer simply watching the characters and telling the reader about what they do – like a film camera?
iii) Does the writer look into the characters' minds and tell the reader what they are thinking?
iv) Does the writer make comments about his characters – does he tell the reader what to think?

If you intend to write, it may be worth deciding which technique you will use. There are many more, of course. A writer may pretend to be lots of different characters and some books are written as though by more than one person. See Paul Zindel's THE PIGMAN for example. Ask yourself the above questions about a book you have read recently – which standpoint did the writer take?

Standpoints

Here are some examples of different standpoints. All these passages deal with a man meeting a woman but the styles vary a lot. In each case, write down a brief note to describe the intended relationship between writer, reader and characters.

> I looked up the blue-carpeted foyer at the cluster of girls gossiping outside the Ladies, and saw them part to let Liz through. Some of them stared after her. I noticed, not for the first time, how scruffy she was in her old suede jacket and her dusty black skirt, and it occurred to me that I had rarely, if ever, seen her wearing anything else .... She came and stood beside me, by the showcases. 'Miss Strad-houghton', she said mechanically. 'They gave the title to

the wrong girl', I said with a clumsy attempt at gallantry.

We strolled away from the Roxy and the block of tobacconist's shops, chemists and hairdressers that was built in with it, and over the waste ground to the New Road. We walked up New Road past the Houghtondale Arms, the bus sheds and the crematorium and then, where the dump of cracked drainpipes and the crusty little hills of tar marked the last gasp of housing development, we turned into the unadopted road that led down into Foley Bottoms.

At some point during the evening, probably in the flight from the pub concert-room, I had started walking like a man with flat feet, and I was trying hard to stop it. 'Do you find life complicated?' I said as we walked along. I was long past caring one way or the other about anything very much, and what I said was the first thing that came into my head.

'Hmm-hmm', said Liz happily.

I said: 'I wish it was something you could tear up and start again. Life, I mean. You know, like starting a new page in an exercise book.'

'Well, it's been done', said Liz. 'Turning over a new leaf.'

'I turn over a new leaf every day,' I said. 'But the blots

show through'. I was rather pleased with this.

We came to the end of the unadopted road and crossed over the broken-down chestnut fencing and the backwash of old bricks and bottles that was the entrance to Foley Bottoms.

'Why are you walking like that?' said Liz.

'Like what?'

'Sort of leaning forward as though you were on roller skates.'

About half a dozen selected falsehoods skimmed through my mind, ranging from bad shoes to middle ear disease. 'I'm pretending I've got flat feet', I said at length.

'Fathead.'

from BILLY LIAR by Keith Waterhouse

'It was the waiting.'

'It was.'

They stood on the platform. A line of trolleys rattled by, and people moved, but Tom and Jan held each other invisible.

'Checking.'

'What?'

'Memory: hair in my face.'

'You.'

'And you.'

'It was waiting.'

They had to step back to be closer.

'Let me look at you', said Tom.

'You're too far away.'

'Your fault.'

They came together again.

'Are your eyes shut?'

'Yes.'

'Funny. I shut my eyes to be with you when I'm not, and when I am –'

'You shut them!'

They giggled, and went the length of Crewe station, skipping, running, breaking to rejoin, under the glass, the dark bridge and into the daylight to the platform's tip, and back again. The platform made a headland above the woven lines, and at the end, away from passengers, was an old bench. Tom and Jan sat there in the sunlight and wind and watched the junction.

'Like Blackpool prom, isn't it?'

'Quieter.'

'Coffee?' said Jan.

'Yes.'

They returned to the gloom and the announcements and people, trains drawing hands apart.

'Don't look', said Tom.

They sat in the cafeteria and drank their coffee.

from RED SHIFT by Alan Garner

While he watched the far-removed landscape a tawny stain grew into being on the lower verge: the eclipse had begun. This marked a preconcerted moment, for the remote celestial phenomenon had been pressed into service as a lover's signal. Yeobright's mind flew back to earth at the sight; he arose, shook himself, and listened. Minute after minute passed by, perhaps ten minutes passed, and the shadow on the moon perceptibly widened. He heard a rustling on his left hand, a cloaked figure with an upturned face appeared at the base of the Barrow, and Clym descended. In a moment the figure was in his arms, and his lips upon hers.

'My Eustacia!'

'Clym, dearest!'

Such a situation had less than three months brought forth.

They remained long without a single utterance, for no language could reach the level of their condition: words were as the rusty implements of a by-gone barbarous epoch, and only to be occasionally tolerated.

'I began to wonder why you did not come', said Yeobright, when she had withdrawn a little from his embrace.

'You said ten minutes after the first mark of shade on the edge of the moon; and that's what it is now.'

'Well, let us only think that here we are.'

Then, holding each other's hands, they were again silent and the shadow on the moon's disc grew a little larger.

from THE RETURN OF THE NATIVE by Thomas Hardy

... She is beginning to cry: her heart has swelled so, the tears stand in her eyes; she gives one great sob, while the corners of her mouth quiver, and the tears roll down.

She doesn't know that there is another turning to the Hermitage, that she is close against it, and that Arthur Donnithorne is only a few yards from her, full of one thought, and a thought of which she only is the object. He is going to see Hetty again: that is the longing which has been growing through the last three hours to a feverish thirst. Not, of course, to speak in the caressing way into which he had unguardedly fallen before dinner, but to set things right with her by a kindness which would have the air of friendly civility, and prevent her from running away with wrong notions about their mutual relation.

If Hetty had known he was there, she would not have cried; and it would have been better, for then Arthur would perhaps have behaved as wisely as he had intended. As it was, she started when he appeared at the end of the side-alley, and looked up at him with two great drops rolling down her cheeks. What else could he do but speak to her in a soft, soothing tone, as if she were a bright-eyed spaniel with a thorn in her foot?

'Has something frightened you, Hetty? Have you seen anything in the wood? Don't be frightened – I'll take care of you now.'

Hetty was blushing so, she didn't know whether she was happy or miserable. To be crying again – what did gentlemen think of girls who cried in that way? She felt unable even to say 'no', but could only look away from him and wipe the tears from her cheek. Not before a great drop had fallen on her rose-coloured strings – she knew that quite well.

'Come, be cheerful again. Smile at me and tell me what's the matter. Come, tell me.'

Hetty turned her head towards him, whispered, 'I thought you wouldn't come', and slowly got courage to lift her eyes to him. That look was too much: he must have had eyes of Egyptian granite not to look too lovingly in return.

'You little frightened bird! Little tearful rose! Silly pet! You won't cry again, now I'm with you, will you?'

Ah, he doesn't know in the least what he is saying. This is not what he meant to say. His arm is stealing round the waist again, it is tightening its clasp; he is bending his face nearer and nearer to the round cheek; his lips are meeting those pouting child-lips and for a long moment time has vanished.

from ADAM BEDE by George Eliot

Study the passages in N2 to see how important **dialogue** is in narrative, and also **description**. These things are often present in a story and the story is better because of them – if what is said and what is described are carefully chosen.

Suspense and climax

A story must come to life when it is told. An exciting moment must be carefully recounted if the reader is to enjoy the experience of reading. **Suspense** and **climax** must play a large part in a story which intends to be exciting. Study the following passage to see how these techniques can work:

He slipped through the side streets, showing his police pass to take a short cut, and emerged in the Rue de Rennes. It was the same story; the road was blocked off two hundred metres from the square, the crowds massed behind the barriers, the street empty except for the patrolling CRS men. He started asking again.

Seen anyone? No, sir. Any one been past, anyone at all? No, sir. Down in the forecourt of the station he heard the band of the Garde Republicaine tuning their instruments. He glanced at his watch. The General would be arriving

any time now. Seen anybody pass, anyone at all? No, sir.
Not this way. All right, carry on.

Down in the square he heard a shouted order, and from
one end of the Boulevard de Montparnasse a motorcade
swept into the Place du 18 Juin. He watched it turn into
the gates of the station forecourt, police erect and at the
salute. All eyes down the street were watching the sleek black
cars. The crowd behind the barrier a few yards from him
strained to get through. He looked up at the roof-tops.
Good boys. The watchers of the roof ignored the spectacle
below them; their eyes never stopped flickering across the
roof-tops and windows across the road from where they
crouched on the parapets, watching for a slight movement
at a window.

He had reached the western side of the Rue de Rennes.
A young CRS man stood with his feet planted squarely in
the gap where the last steel crowd barrier abutted the wall
of number 132. He flashed his card at the man, who stiffened.

'Anybody passed this way?'

'No, sir.'

'How long have you been here?'

'Since twelve o'clock, sir, when the street was closed.'

'Nobody been through that gap?'

'No, sir. Well ... only the old cripple, and he lives down
there.'

'What cripple?'

'Oldish chap, sir. Looked sick as a dog. He had his ID card,
and Mutilé de Guerre card. Address given as 154 Rue de
Rennes. Well, I had to let him through, sir. He looked all
in, real sick. Not surprised with him in that greatcoat, and
in this weather and all. Daft, really.'

'Greatcoat?'

'Yessir. Great long coat. Military like the old soldiers used
to wear. Too hot for this weather, though.'

'What was wrong with him?'

'Well, he was too hot, wasn't he, sir?'

'You said he was a war-wounded. What was wrong with
him?'

'One leg, sir. Only one leg. Hobbling along he was, on
a crutch.'

From down in the square the first clear peals from the
trumpets sounded. 'Come, children of the Motherland, the
day of glory has arrived ...' Several of the crowd took up
the familiar chant of 'La Marseillaise'.

'Crutch?' To himself, Lebel's voice seemed a small thing,

very far away. The CRS man looked at him solicitously.

'Yessir. A crutch, like one-legged men always have. An aluminium crutch ...'

Lebel was haring off down the street yelling at the CRS man to follow him.

They were drawn up in the sunlight in a hollow square. The cars were parked nose to tail along the wall of the station façade. Directly opposite the cars, along the railings that separated the forecourt from the square, were the ten recipients of the medals to be distributed by the Head of State. On the east side of the forecourt were the officials and diplomatic corps, a solid mass of charcoal-grey suiting, with here and there the red rosebud of the Legion of Honour.

The western side was occupied by the serried red plumes and burnished casques of the Garde Republicaine, the band-men standing a little out in front of the guard of honour itself.

Round one of the cars up against the station façade clustered a group of protocol officials and palace staff. The band started to play 'La Marseillaise'.

The Jackal raised the rifle and squinted down into the forecourt. He picked the war veteran nearest to him, the man who would be the first to get his medal. He was a short, stocky man, standing very erect. His head came clearly into the sight, almost a complete profile. In a few minutes, facing this man about one foot taller, would be another face, proud, arrogant, topped by a khaki kepi adorned with two gold stars on the front.

'Marchons, marchons, a la victoire ...' Boom-ba-boom. The last notes of the National Anthem died away, replaced by a great silence. The roar of the Commander of the Guard echoed across the station yard. 'General Salute ... Pres-e-e-ent arms.' There were three precise crashes as white-gloved hands smacked in unison across rifle-butts and magazines, and heels came down together. The crowd around the car parted, falling back in two halves. From the centre a single tall figure emerged and began to stalk towards the line of war veterans. At fifty metres from them the rest of the crowd stopped, except the Minister of Ancient Combatants, who would introduce the veterans to their President, and an official carrying a velvet cushion with a row of ten pieces of metal and ten coloured ribbons on it. Apart from these two, Charles de Gaulle marched forward alone.

'This one?'

Lebel stopped, panting, and gestured towards a doorway.

'I think so, sir. Yes, this was it, second from the end. This was where he came in.'

The little detective was gone down the hallway, and Valremy followed him, not displeased to be out of the street, where their odd behaviour in the middle of a serious occasion was attracting disapproving frowns from the higher brass standing at attention against the railings of the station yard. Well, if he was put on the carpet, he could always say that the funny little man had posed as a Commissaire of Police, and that he had been trying to detain him.

When he got into the hall the detective was shaking the door of the concierge's parlour.

'Where's the concierge?' he yelled.

'I don't know, sir.'

Before he could protest, the little man had smashed the frosted-glass panel with his elbow, reached inside and opened the door.

'Follow me', he called, and dashed inside.

'Too bloody right I'm going to follow you', thought Valremy. 'You're off your chump.'

He found the little detective at the door of the scullery. Looking over the man's shoulder he saw the concierge tied up on the floor, still unconscious.

'Blimey.' Suddenly it occurred to him the little man was not joking. He was a Police Commissaire, and they were after a criminal. This was the big moment he had dreamed of, and he wished he was back in barracks.

'Top floor', shouted the detective, and was gone up the stairs with a speed that surprised Valremy, who pounded after him, unslinging his carbine as he ran.

The President of France paused before the first man in the line of veterans and stooped slightly to listen to the Minister explain who he was and what was his citation for valour shown on that day nineteen years before. When the Minister had finished he inclined his head towards the veteran, turned towards the man with the cushion, and took the proffered medal. As the band began a softly played rendering of 'La Marjolaine' the tall General pinned the medal on to the rounded chest of the elderly man in front of him. Then he stepped back for the salute.

Six floors up and a hundred and thirty metres away the Jackal held the rifle very steady and squinted down the telescopic sight. He could see the features quite clearly, the brow shaded by the peak of the kepi, the peering eyes, the prow-like nose. He saw the raised saluting hand come down from the peak of the cap, the crossed wires of the sight were spot on the exposed temple. Softly, gently, he squeezed the trigger ...

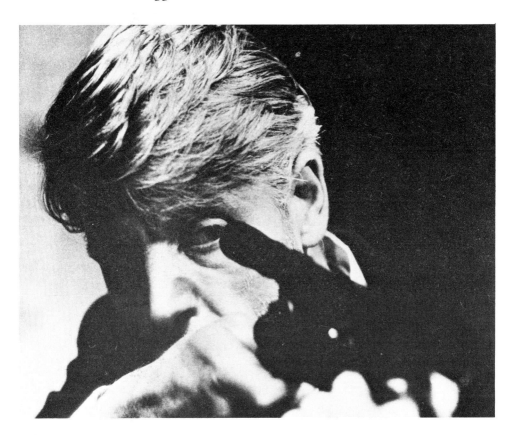

A split second later he was staring down into the station forecourt as if he could not believe his eyes. Before the bullet had passed out of the end of the barrel, the President of France had snapped his head forward without warning. As the assassin watched in disbelief, he solemnly planted a kiss on each cheek of the man in front of him. As he himself was a foot taller, he had had to bend forward and down to give the traditional kiss of congratulation that is habitual among the French and certain other nations, but which baffles Anglo-Saxons.

It was later established the bullet had passed a fraction of an inch behind the moving head. Whether the President heard the whipcrack from the sound barrier, travelling on a narrow line down the flight path of the bullet, is not known. He gave no sign of it. The Minister and the official heard nothing; neither did those fifty metres away.

The slug tore into the sun-softened tarmacadam of the forecourt, its disintegration taking place harmlessly inside more than an inch of tar. 'La Marjolaine' played on. The President, after planting the second kiss, straightened up and moved sedately on towards the next man.

Behind his gun, the Jackal started to swear, softly, venomously. He had never missed a stationary target at a hundred and fifty yards in his life before. Then he calmed down; there was still time. He tore open the breech of the rifle, ejecting the spent cartridge to fall harmlessly on to the carpet. Taking the second one off the table he pushed it home and closed the breech.

Claude Lebel arrived panting on the sixth floor. He thought his heart was going to come out of his chest and roll all over the landing. There were two doors leading towards the front of the building. He looked from one to the other as the CRS man joined him, submachine carbine held on his hip, pointing forward. As Lebel hesitated in front of the two doors, from behind one of them came a low but distinct 'Phut'. Lebel pointed at the door lock with his forefinger.

'Shoot it off', he ordered, and stepped back. The CRS man braced himself on both feet and fired. Bits of wood, metal and spent, flattened slugs flew in all directions. The door buckled and swung drunkenly inwards. Valremy was first into the room, Lebel on his heels.

Valremy could recognise the grey tufts of hair, but that was all. The man had two legs, the greatcoat was gone, and the forearms that gripped the rifle were on a strong young man. The gunman gave him no time; rising from his seat behind the table, swinging in one smooth motion at a half-crouch, he fired from the hip. The single bullet made no sound; the echoes of Valremy's gun-burst were still ringing in his ears. The slug from the rifle tore into his chest, struck the sternum and exploded. There was a feeling of tearing and ripping and of great sudden stabs of pain; then even they were gone. The light faded as if summer had turned to winter.

A piece of carpet came up and smacked him on the cheek, except that it was his cheek that was lying on the carpet. The loss of feeling swept up through the thighs and belly, then the chest and neck. The last thing he remembered was a salty taste in the mouth, like he had had after bathing in the sea at Kermadec, and a one-legged old gull sitting on a post. Then it was all dark.

Above his body Claude Lebel stared into the eyes of the other man. He had no trouble with his heart; it did not seem to be pumping any more.

'Chacal', he said. The other man said simply 'Lebel'. He was fumbling with the gun, tearing open the breech. Lebel saw the glint as the cartridge case dropped to the floor. The man swept something off the table and stuffed it into the breech. His grey eyes were still staring at Lebel.

He's trying to fix me rigid, thought Lebel with a sense of unrealism. He's going to shoot. He's going to kill me.

With an effort he dropped his eyes to the floor. The boy from the CRS had fallen sideways: his carbine had slipped from his fingers and lay at Lebel's feet. Without conscious thought he dropped to his knees, grabbed the MAT 49, swinging it upwards with one hand, the other clawing for the trigger. He heard the Jackal snap home the breech of the rifle as he found the trigger of the carbine. He pulled it.

The roar of the exploding ammunition filled the small room and was heard in the square. Later press enquiries were met with the explanation that it had been a motor-cycle with a faulty silencer which some ass had kicked into life a few streets away at the height of the ceremony. Half a magazine full of nine-millimetre bullets hit the Jackal in the chest, picked him up, half-turned him in the air and slammed his body into an untidy heap in the far corner near the sofa. As he fell, he brought the standard lamp with him. Down below, the band struck up 'Mon Regiment et Ma Patrie'.

from THE DAY OF THE JACKAL by Frederick Forsyth

What is happening in this passage? Perhaps you could jot down the sequence of events in order.

Notice how the writer changes scene and focus. What effect does this have?

Can you use the same techniques yourself? Try to build a climactic narrative like the one above.

Suggestions for writing

N5

You may be well advised to select the details you include in a narrative and, as always, your selection will depend on many things, including a sense of the audience you are aiming at.

Some writers, though, would say that you should not select, that life is a confusion of thoughts, feelings, sights, sounds, smells, actions, speech, and that it should be recorded in this way. Read the following passage and then try your hand at the same technique, which is sometimes called 'stream of consciousness'. Do you find any advantages in this technique?

> His hand took his hat from the peg over his initialled heavy overcoat, and his lost property office secondhand waterproof. Stamps; stickback pictures. Daresay lots of officers are in the swim too. Course they do. The sweated legend in the crown of his hat told him mutely: Plasto's high grade ha. He peeped quickly inside the leather headband. White slip of paper. Quite safe.
>
> On the doorstep, he felt in his hip pocket for the latch key. Not there. In the trousers I left off. Must get it. Potato I have. Creaky wardrobe. No use disturbing her. She turned over sleepily that time. He pulled the halldoor to after him very quietly, more, till the footleaf dropped gently over the threshold, a limp lid. Looked shut. All right till I come back anyhow.
>
> He crossed to the bright side, avoiding the loose cellar-flap of number seventy-five. The sun was nearing the steeple of George's church. Be a warm day I fancy. Specially in these black clothes feel it more. Black conducts, reflects (refracts is it?), the heat. But I couldn't go in that light suit. Make a picnic of it. His eyelids sank quietly often as he walked in happy warmth. Boland's breadvan delivering with trays our daily but she prefers yesterday's loaves turnovers crisp crowns hot. Makes you feel young. Somewhere in the east: early morning: set off at dawn, travel round in front of the sun, steal a day's march on him. Keep it up for ever never grow a day older technically, walk along a strange, strange, come to a city gate, sentry there, old ranker too, old Tweedy's big moustaches leaning on a long kind of spear. Wander through awned streets. Turbaned faces going by. Dark caves of carpet shops, big man, Turko the terrible,

seated cross-legged smoking a coiled pipe. Cries of sellers in the streets. Drink water scented with fennel; sherbet. Wander along all day. Might meet a robber or two. Well, meet him. Getting on to sundown. The shadows of the mosques along the pillars: priest with a scroll rolled up. A shiver of the trees, signal, the evening wind. I pass on. Fading gold sky. A mother watches from her doorway. She calls her children home in their dark language. High wall: beyond strings twanged. Night sky moon, violet colour of Molly's new garters. Strings, listen. A girl playing one of these instruments what do you call them: dulcimers. I pass.

Probably not a bit like it really. Kind of stuff you read: in the track of the sun. Sunburst on the titlepage. He smiled, pleasing himself.

from ULYSSES by James Joyce

Can you tell what is happening in the passage above? How does each idea lead into the next? Try writing a stream of consciousness narrative based on thoughts of your own.

Perhaps this poem might suggest a story. From whose point of view would you write it?

DETECTIVE STORY

The Stranger left the house in the small hours;
A neighbour heard his steps between two dreams;
The body was discovered strewn with flowers;
Their evenings were too passionate, it seems.

They used to be together quite a lot;
The friend was dressed in black, distinguished looking
The porter said; his wife had always thought
They were so nice and interested in cooking.

And this was true perhaps. The other night
They made a soup that was a great success;
They drank some lager too and all was right,
The talk, the kisses and at last the chess.

'It was great fun!' they said; yet their true love
Throbbed in their breasts like pus that must be freed
The porter found the weapon and the glove,
But only our despair can find the creed.

Demetrios Capetanakis

N8

One of the earliest forms of storytelling, in the days before writing, was the ballad. This was a rhyming song, told around a fire, maybe, with a chorus, in four line verses, focussing on small incidents in the story. This example was written in modern times. Decide what is happening and build a story around it.

O WHAT IS THAT SOUND?

O what is that sound that so thrills the ear,
  Down in the valley drumming, drumming?
Only the scarlet soldiers, dear,
  The soldiers coming.

O what is that light I see flashing so clear,
  Over the distance brightly, brightly?
Only the sun on their weapons, dear
  As they step lightly.

O what are they doing with all that gear,
  What are they doing this morning, this morning?
Only their usual manoeuvres, dear,
  Or perhaps a warning.

O why have they left the road down there,
  Why are they suddenly wheeling, wheeling?
Perhaps a change in their orders dear,
  Why are you kneeling?

O haven't they stopped for the doctor's care,
  Haven't they reined their horses, their horses?
Why, they are none of them wounded, dear,
  None of these forces.

O is it the parson they want, with white hair,
  Is it the parson, is it, is it?
No, they are passing his gateway, dear,
  Without a visit.

O it must be the farmer who lives so near,
  It must be the farmer, so cunning, so cunning?
They have passed the farmyard already, dear,
  And now they are running.

O where are you going? Stay with me here!
  Were the vows you swore deceiving, deceiving?
No, I promised to love you, dear,
  But I must be leaving.

O it's broken the lock and splintered the door,
  O it's the gate where they're turning, turning
Their boots are heavy on the floor
  And their eyes are burning.

W. H. Auden

N9

Try writing your own ballad, perhaps based on a newspaper headline or this report. Write the ballad in four-line verses of regular rhythm, the first line to rhyme with the third, and the second with the fourth. Obviously, you must plan the story beforehand and only select the most important incidents and details for inclusion in the ballad.

SWEETHEARTS ELOPE AFTER BAN ON LOVE

Police all over Britain were last night looking for two runaway lovers, Tim Brown, sixteen, and his schoolgirl sweetheart Jane Smith. They disappeared after Jane's parents had shown disapproval of their romance.

N10

Use this sequence of photographs as the basis for a narrative.

N11

Remember that lively writing depends on an ability to recreate vivid experiences. Look carefully at these examples and see if you can write something in a similar fashion.

I ate the end of my piece of cheese and took a swallow of wine. Through the other noise I heard a cough, then came the chuh-chuh-chuh-chuh – then there was flash, as a blast-furnace door is swung open, and a roar that started white and went red and on and on in a rushing wind. I tried to breathe but my breath would not come and I felt myself rush bodily out of myself and out and out and out and all the time bodily in the wind. I went out swiftly, all of myself and I knew I was dead and that it had all been a mistake to think you just died. Then I floated, and instead of going on I felt myself slide back. I breathed and I was back. The ground was torn up and in front of my head there was a splintered beam of wood. In the jolt of my head I heard somebody crying. I thought somebody was screaming. I tried to move but I could not move. I heard the machine-guns and rifles firing across the river and all along the river. There was a great splashing and I saw the star-shells go up and burst and float whitely and rockets going up and heard the bombs, all this in a moment, and then I heard close to me someone saying, 'Mamma mia! Oh, mamma mia!' I pulled and twisted and got my legs loose finally and turned around and touched him. It was Passini and when I touched him he screamed. His legs were toward me and I saw in the dark and the light that they were both smashed above the knee. One leg was gone and the other was held by tendons and part of the trouser and the stump twitched and jerked as though it were not connected. He bit his arm and moaned, 'Oh, mamma mia, mamma mia', then, 'Dio ti salvi, Maria. Dio ti salvi, Maria. Oh Jesus shoot me Christ shoot me, Mamma mia, mamma mia, oh purest lovely Mary shoot me. Stop it. Stop it. Stop it. Oh Jesus lovely Mary stop it. Oh oh oh oh', then choking, 'Mamma mamma mia.' Then he was quiet, biting his arm, the stump of his leg twitching.

from A FAREWELL TO ARMS by Ernest Hemingway

By mid-morning I was in a state of developing madness, possessed by pounding deliriums of thirst, my brain running and reeling through all the usual obsessions that are said to accompany the man in the desert. Fantasies of water rose up and wrapped me in cool wet leaves, or pressed the thought of cucumber peel across my stinging eyes and filled my mouth with dripping moss. I began to drink monsoons and winter mists, to lick up the first fat drops of thunder, to lie down naked on deep-sea sponges and rub my lips against the scales of fish. I saw the steamy, damp-uddered cows of home planting their pink-lily mouths in the brook, then standing, knee-deep among dragonflies, whipping the reeds with their tasselled tails. Images bubbled up green from valleys of shining rain and fields of storm-crushed grass, with streams running down from the lime-cold hills into buttery swamps of flowers. I heard my mother again in her summer kitchen splashing water on garden salads, heard the gulping gush of the garden pump and swans' wings beating the lake ...

The rest of the day was a blur. I remember seeing the spire of a church rising from the plain like the jet of a fountain. Then there was a shower of eucalyptus trees brushing against a roadside tavern, and I was at a bar calling for bottles of pop ...

The first mouthful of mineral water burst in my throat and cascaded like frosted stars. Then I was given a plate of ham, several glasses of sherry, and a deep languor spread through my limbs. I remember no more of my benefactors, or what they said; only the drowsy glories of drinking. Later, much later, I was lifted to my feet and half-led, half-carried outside.

from AS I WALKED OUT ONE MIDSUMMER MORNING
by Laurie Lee

In all cases, start your narrative well, make sure you bring the incidents to life and decide on the relationship you are going to have with your characters and your readers.

REPORTING
AND RECORDING

The newspapers

R1 Bring in some copies of the most popular daily newspapers. How do they differ? Are they meant for different audiences? If so, which paper is designed for whom?

R2 Design a questionnaire to carry out a limited survey among parents, pupils and teachers. Try to find out why people choose one particular newspaper and who they expect to read the others. What do they think of the news topics covered by each newspaper and the standard of reporting?

R3 Can you make any judgements about the standard of reporting in newspapers? Compare the following reports, both dealing with the same event. How do they differ in fact, style, vocabulary and emphasis?

TV CHAMP BRIAN OUT OF FINAL

By STEVE BAILEY

BRIAN JACKS, the judo expert who became a sporting cult figure on TV's Superstars, is out of the world finals.

Cockney Brian, who was Britain's brightest hope for the contest in Bermuda next month, has shingles and a blood disorder.

Brian, 32, said yesterday: 'I'm sorry but I can't go on. I've fought against it, tried to keep my training up, but this time I'm beaten.'

Record-beater

Brian took the contest by the scruff of the neck earlier this year and helped hoist the programme into the BBC's Top Ten.

European Superstars records tumbled as he:
● Almost doubled the previous best for arm dips . . . with seventy-six in 60 seconds.
● Shaved nearly three seconds off the 120 metres canoeing record of 37 seconds.
● Clipped half a second off the 200 metres cycling event with a time of 13.45 seconds.

Brian, four times European judo champion, will now miss the chance of picking up £20,000 in prize money.

He said 'The money is not the main thing. I was doing this for Britain. But I do not want to go if I'm less than 110 per cent fit.'

Brian has been ordered to take a complete rest at his home in Orpington, Kent. A spokesman for the BBC said: 'It is extremely sad. The public and the BBC have really taken Brian to heart and we rated his chances.'

Brian's replacement will be Dave 'Boy' Green, European welterweight boxing champion.

THE SUNDAY MIRROR 25 February 1979

Jacks not all right

BRIAN JACKS, the judo man, whose fighting qualities on BBC TV's 'Superstars' programme have sent audience ratings soaring and won him £2,500 as joint European champion, is out of the running for the world title. Jacks will compete when the world final is filmed in Freetown, Bahamas, in a fortnight, but a severe attack of shingles has left him seriously unfit. He has trained little since Christmas, (and that little against medical advice) and recently he could not even complete a one-mile run. But with a £12,500 first prize on offer Jacks, who has just signed away his Olympic medal hopes for an advertising agreement with a sporting-goods manufacturer, cannot be deterred. He plans to drop out of the stamina events of 800 metres and cycling, and put all his efforts into the sprints and strength tests. 'How can I pull out now?' he says. 'When will I ever get another chance to win this sort of cash?'

THE OBSERVER 25 February 1979

R4 The reports of football matches are open to a great deal of criticism because they are prone to repetition and cliché. Why should this be? Think of as many reasons as possible.

R5 What clichés do you associate with football reports? Can you find any in the daily papers?

R6 Study these descriptions of footballers scoring goals and discuss how best to avoid falling into the trap of repetition or cliché.

a) After Swain's jinking run down the left wing, Peters' cross was met solidly by a scoring header from the ebullient Johnson.

b) Brown's weak punch was gathered by Jones on the edge of the area and, before the defence could recover, he powered the ball into the back of the net.

c) Watson was put through by Collins with only five minutes to spare. The big striker drew goalkeeper Ferris, eluded his despairing attempt to block, and sidefooted home.

d) Daneman settled it just after half time with the third, his opportunist volley glancing off a defender and scraping in off the underside of the woodwork.

R7

Would you say that the following is a successful report? What do you think of the style in which it is written?

United Sweep to their Title

West Ham 1   Manchester United 6

A monumental performance by Manchester United confirmed them in their Championship, virtually obliterated West Ham, and left London with the marvellous concluding statement from Matt Busby's team that if the capital is to have the Cup Final then Manchester is once again the centre of the universe.

For the ragged, ragamuffin red-and-white battalions which invaded the field at the end, screaming for Busby, there has never been any doubt about that. United had clearly spurned the thought of scrambling the solitary point they needed. They devastated West Ham with the intent, with the power, the pace, the professionalism of their play from the beginning.

A Charlton goal in the second minute, then three in ten minutes, left West Ham demoralized, concussed, and, at the heart of a ravishing first-half performance, stood Bobby Charlton. His goal was astonishing in its speed, its audacity, and the lightning reaction which Charlton displayed on siezing at a quarter-chance.

Law cut Stiles through perfectly. Stiles was blocked, the ball broke loose but offered only the tightest of chances. Charlton went at it with a feverish venom that seemed almost out of character, thrashing the ball irrevocably past Mackleworth for a quite sensational goal.

Bobby Charlton, probably the best-loved player in our game, went on to play a first half that surpassed even his performance against Portugal in the World Cup semi-final. His touch on the ball, delicate and stunning, his control (once he turned past seven successive West Ham players with the same move, that quick flick with the outside of his left foot), his command of the entire mid-field when he chose—here was a vintage performance from a most wonderfully gifted player at the very height of his maturity.

THE OBSERVER 7 May 1967

R8

Arrange to watch a football match (either 'live' or the television highlights) and write a report on it afterwards. Compare your version with those in the newspapers on the following morning.

Is it possible to find original expression in such a report?
Is 'trying to be different' a mistake?

A well-rounded view

R9

Reporters can easily be accused of bias. They may not express their own opinions strongly, but they can choose both the details that they include in an article and the people whom they interview. Bias, however, runs contrary to a tradition of 'objective' reporting which tries to allow conflicting views to be expressed fairly and equally. Do you think that this is a worthwhile ideal to pursue?

R10

Discuss how a headline or a 'news-slant' can be misleading about a certain event. Try to collect examples over a period of time.

R11

If an article were to appear under the headline:

SCHOOLGIRL SENT HOME FOR NOT WEARING UNIFORM

how would the reporter approach his work?
Who would he interview?
How might he have been put on to the story?

Invent some interviews and facts and then write this imaginary news story. Choose your own headline. Try to give a fair and balanced view of the facts.

R12

Have you been fair? Allow a group of your friends to analyse and criticise your article.

R13

Improvise a scene in which the following chain of events takes place:

a) A pupil refuses to do his homework.
b) The pupil is sent to the Head Teacher.
c) The Head consults the parents, who say they do not believe in homework.

d) The Head suspends the pupil.

e) The pupil is forced to stay at home and the parents complain to the press.

R14

Send in reporters to interview those involved. Should anyone else be asked for their views?

Edit the interviews and write a balanced article.

R15

An accident takes place near a primary school. A small child is badly injured by a speeding car before the traffic warden has come on duty. There have been previous protests to the council demanding a reduction in the speed limit here from 50 mph to 30 mph following three earlier accidents at the same spot.

As a local reporter, how would you set about compiling an article for the paper? Who should you interview?
Write the article together with an explanation of the steps you took.

R16

If reporting and recording appeals to you, it might be possible to start a small school (or community) newspaper or magazine portraying local life. If you decide to experiment with such a project, an arranged visit to your local newspaper office might provide invaluable help.

Recording for other purposes

HISTORICAL

R17

The recording of important historical events has long ceased to be just a listing of known facts. Very often, historical accounts contain a surprising amount of detail.

The following is taken from a modern account of the battle of Culloden in which Bonny Prince Charlie was routed by the English army. This extract deals with the march of the English from Nairn towards the Scots:

The men and boys of the Main Guard drums came to the ready: left heel in the hollow of the right foot, and left knee bent so that the drum was well balanced, elbows up and buttons of the sticks level with the white horse of Hanover on each cap. At four o'clock, from Nairn a mile away, there came the signal rattle of a single drum, and immediately the sticks of the Main Guard came down on the skins in the drag and paradiddle of the General, the left hand striking a regular, remorseless beat. The drummers moved off from the Main Guard tent, each man marching, beating, towards his own battalion streets. In Nairn the orderly drummer of the Duke's Guard, who had given the signal, strutted from the bridge to the Horologe Stone, and the noise of his sticks sounded again on the narrow windows of the town. The anger of all the drums rolled westward on the wind down the valley of the Nairn, and was heard there by the vedettes of Kingston's Horse. At the alarm-pieces, set forward of the artillery park, a duty gunner in a plain blue coat lowered his linstock to the touch-holes. The discharge of the two guns was muffled by the rain-soaked air, but this, too, the thankful outposts heard, and they turned their horses towards camp, riding through the water at Kildrummie ...

So the King's Army in Scotland marched, a scarlet and white animal crawling over the dead brown heather at two and a half miles an hour. And blind at its centre, where each red cell that was a man saw only the greased hair and leather stock of the man in front of him. At its head, too, it was little better than blind. There, mounted men in gold lace and powdered wigs knew nothing but what they might be told by the forty troopers of Kingston's Horse and the Campbell scouts in skirmish line advanced. The grey sky seemed to press down as the daylight grew, and the raw wind was thickening with rain.

from CULLODEN by John Prebble

a) Why have such precise details been included?
b) What is the effect of these details on the reader?
c) How do you think the historian gathered such a wide variety of information – where would he have found such details?

This photograph may help you to reconstruct conditions in the trenches during the 1914–18 war.

R18

It might be possible for you to carry out your own historical reporting. Perhaps you can find one or more people who were present at a famous event (during the last war or, less dramatic, in a protest demonstration of recent years, for example). Interview the witness, carrying out the following tasks:

a) Prepare your questions in advance, aiming to gather details which you think important in understanding what it was like to be there.

b) Read other accounts of the incident or any documents connected with it.

c) Try to visit some of the places involved or carry out some of the activities which took place. (Like running up a beach in the case of a water-borne, armed landing, for example.)

d) Carry out any other research which may give you an insight into what it was like to be there.

Write a detailed account of the event using all the knowledge you have gained.

SCIENTIFIC

R19

Experiment to test the conditions needed for Pepsin action

Method

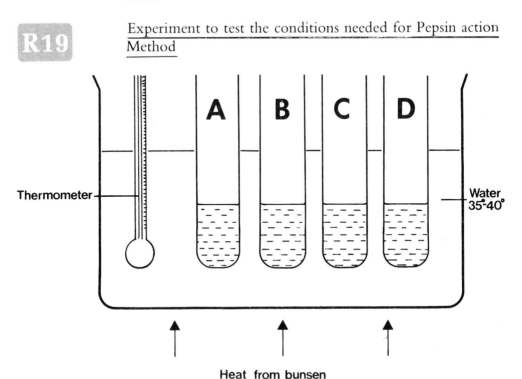

Heat from bunsen

2cm³ of eggwhite was added to four test tubes which were then placed into a water bath maintained at 35°–40°C. When the eggwhite had reached this temperature the following extra contents were simultaneously added to the tubes as labelled:

A : 1 cm³ of pepsin.

B : 12 drops of hydrochloric acid.

C : 1 cm³ of pepsin plus 12 drops of hydrochloric acid.

D : 1 cm³ of previously boiled pepsin plus 12 drops of hydrochloric acid.

The test tubes were left for 15–20 minutes, after which time the clarity of the tube contents was noted. (Undigested eggwhite protein split into separate amino acid goes clear.)

Results

	Time (m)	Clarity
Test Tube A	20	Cloudy
Test Tube B	20	Cloudy
Test Tube C	20	Clear
Test Tube D	20	Cloudy

Conclusion

The experiment indicated that the enzyme pepsin would only act to speed the breakdown of eggwhite protein in an acidic medium. (Test tube D also showed that enzymes are destroyed by boiling.)

Tubes A and D acted as *controls* to illustrate that the eggwhite would not break down with only pepsin or hydrochloric acid but needed a combination of both.

R20

Compare the above account of an experiment with the one below. Which version is the best for its purpose? Why? What is the purpose of writing up an experiment?

On Monday I went to biology and had to do an experiment with the liquid called pepsin, which is an enzyme. We used four test tubes filled with eggwhite. I put pepsin in one, acid in another and John put pepsin *and* acid in another. In the fourth one we put *boiled* pepsin and acid. Then we let them stand for twenty minutes while I read about pepsin in a book.

John kept the time and, after twenty minutes, we looked at the test tubes. All were cloudy except the third and I asked the teacher the reason for this. He said that it was because the pepsin and the acid broke up the eggwhite protein. You need the pepsin and the acid before you can do this.

PERSUASION

Seduction

P1

There are a variety of techniques used in persuasion, and these are put to a variety of purposes. Do these two poets share identical aims? How do their techniques differ?

TO HIS COY MISTRESS

Had we but World enough, and Time,
This coyness Lady were no crime.
We would sit down, and think which way
To walk, and pass our long Loves Day.
Thou by the Indian Ganges side
Should'st Rubies find: I by the Tide
Of Humber would complain. I would
Love you ten years before the Flood:
And you should if you please refuse
Till the conversion of the Jews.
My vegetable Love should grow
Vaster than Empires, and more slow.
An hundred years should grow to praise
Thine Eyes, and on thy Forehead Gaze.
Two hundred to adore each Breast:
But thirty thousand to the rest.
An age at least to every part,
And the last age should show your Heart.
For Lady you deserve this State:
Nor would I love at lower rate.
      But at my back I alwaies hear
Times winged Charriot hurrying near:
And yonder all before us lye
Deserts of vast Eternity.
Thy Beauty shall no more be found;
Nor, in thy marble vault, shall sound
My echoing Song: then Worms shall try
That long preserv'd Virginity:
And your quaint Honour turn to dust;
And into ashes all my Lust.
The Grave's a fine and private place,
But none I think do there embrace.
      Now therefore, while the youthful hew
Sits on thy skin like morning dew,
And while thy willing Soul transpires
At every pore with instant Fires,

Now let us sport us while we may;
And now, like am'rous birds of prey,
Rather at once our Time devour,
Than languish in his slow-chapt pow'r.
Let us roll all our Strength, and all
Our sweetness, up into one Ball:
And tear our Pleasures with rough strife,
Thorough the Iron gates of Life.
Thus, though we cannot make our Sun
Stand still, yet we will make him run.

Andrew Marvell

FOR X

When clerks and navvies fondle
  Beside canals their wenches,
In rapture or in coma
  The haunches that they handle,
And the orange moon sits idle
  Above the orchard slanted –
Upon such easy evenings
  We take our loves for granted.

But when, as now, the creaking
  Trees on the hills of London
Like bison charge their neighbours
  In wind that keeps us waking
And in the draught the scalloped
  Lampshade swings a shadow,
We think of love bound over –
  The mortgage on the meadow.

And one lies lonely, haunted
  By limbs he half remembers,
And one, in wedlock, wonders
  Where is the girl he wanted;
And some sit smoking, flicking
  The ash away and feeling
For love gone up like vapour
  Between the floor and ceiling.

But now when winds are curling
  The trees do you come closer,
Close as an eyelid fasten
  My body in darkness, darling;

Switch the light off and let me
Gather you up and gather
The power of trains advancing
Further, advancing further.

Louis MacNeice

P2

In the relationships between men and women, we shouldn't forget how persuasive actions and even looks can be. Do you recognise the emotions expressed below? How else can looks and actions be persuasive? When are they used consciously?

> The very shape of a baby acts as a stimulus, releasing a flood of parental emotion ...
>
> Indeed, the parental response is so strong that it is even unleashed by the sight of non-human objects bearing the same features. Pet animals, dolls, toys, puppets and fictional cartoon characters possessing big eyes, flat faces, rounded shapes and other infantile characteristics, are immediately appealing. Cartoonists and toy-makers exploit this response by exaggerating these characteristics even more, to produce super-infantile images. Also, human adults whose faces happen to be wider and flatter and bigger-eyed than average often benefit from this unconscious reaction. This is why we like 'sex kittens' more than females who are 'catty'. It also partly explains why women sometimes add to their adult appeal by smoothing their skin, with cosmetics, adopting a look of 'wide-eyed innocence', and pouting with their lips and cheeks.
>
> from MANWATCHING by Desmond Morris

Hidden persuasion

P3

In pairs, one person takes on the job of a salesman persuading a customer. Try to vary the articles for sale. If you, as the salesman, don't think much of the article you're selling does it affect your ability to persuade?

P4

When did you last visit a supermarket? Can you remember the layout of the goods in the shop?
Think for a while and then try to draw a rough plan.

Aladdin's cave – the well-stocked supermarket.

It is said that many supermarket managers arrange their goods in such a way as to sell as much as possible.
Have you been in one which conformed to the following pattern?

a) Music, bright lights and colour to 'hypnotise' the customer.

b) Bulky objects near the entrance to encourage the use of a trolley rather than a basket. It's better to have a trolley filled.

c) Biscuits and cakes near the coffee and tea to encourage 'impulse' buying.

d) Sweets and cigarettes close to hand when queuing at the checkout.

e) Articles needing greater sales placed at eye-level.

What tricks did you use in P3?

P6

Sales and sales marketing are, of course, full time occupations and require a great deal of skill. They depend very much, though, on the tricks of advertising. We pretend we're not taken in by them but how true is this? If we mention the following articles, which brand names leap to mind?

toothpaste
cigars
fishfingers
tea
soap powder
baked beans

P7

What made you remember the brand names you listed?
A tune?   A jingle?   A picture?
Because they're the best? If so, how do you know?

P8

If you were to buy a tube of toothpaste, what information would you need in order to choose the right brand for yourself?
How many of the advertisements you remember having seen or read provide the necessary information?

P9

Do the same kind of test with other products. Collect illustrative examples yourself.

P10

What makes a good TV advertisement? Do the best advertisements advertise the best products? What makes you remember one advertisement rather than another?

P11

In 1957, an American called Vance Packard published his book THE HIDDEN PERSUADERS. It deals with many of the methods used by ad-men to sell their products. Read and discuss the extracts on pages 55-58.

An individual candy-making firm that hired its own psychological consultant came up with another strategy: reward yourself. The theory behind this strategy was that children get rewards of candy for being 'a good little boy' or 'good little girl'. Thus at an early age candy becomes etched in young minds as a reward symbol. Armed with this insight the candy-maker began drumming out this message, 'To make that tough job easier – you deserve M & M Candy.' According to the company sales doubled in test areas. Another candy-maker, Lofts, using both the bite-sized and reward insights, began running full-page ads showing such slim, energetic people as Maria Tallchief, the very svelte prima ballerina. She was dancing and reaching for a tiny peice of candy at the same time, if you can conceive of such a thing. It quoted her as saying what a tough job she has keeping herself constantly in trim, which is why she loves 'Lofts Little Aristocrats' for a quick pick-up backstage without getting a 'filled' feeling. Also she loves them at home after a hard night's work. She concludes: 'I love dainty things.' (Meanwhile, Sugar Information Inc., began running a series of full-page ads urging people to try the 'Scientific Nibble' of sweets to control appetite.)

One aspect of juvenile merchandising that intrigued the depth manipulators was the craze or fad. To a casual observer the juvenile craze for cowboys or knights or Davy Crockett* may seem like a cute bit of froth on the surface of American life. To fad-wise merchandisers such manifestations are largely the result of careful manipulation. They can be enormously profitable or disastrously unprofitable, depending on the merchandiser's cunning.

An evidence of how big the business can be is that the Davy Crockett craze of 1955, which gave birth to 300 Davy Crockett products, lured $300,000,000 from American pockets. Big persuasion indeed!

American merchandisers felt a need for a deeper understanding of these craze phenomena so that they could not only share in the profits, but know when to unload. Research

* Davy Crockett was an American hero, identified by a pioneer's outfit of animal skins. The craze for him, supported by clothing sales and TV programmes, was very similar to those for more recent pop stars and sporting heroes. Can you think of any comparable crazes?

was needed to help the manufacturers avoid overestimating the length of the craze. Many were caught with warehouses full of 'raccoon' tails and buckskin fringe when, almost without warning, the Crockett craze lost its lure. One manufacturer said: 'When they die, they die a horrible death.'

This problem of comprehending the craze drew the attention of such motivation experts as Dr. Dichter and Alfred Politz. And TIDE magazine, journal of merchandisers, devoted a major analysis to the craze.

The experts studied the Crockett extravaganza as a case in point and concluded that its success was due to the fact that it had in good measure all of the three essential ingredients of a profitable fad: symbols, carrying device and fulfilment of a sub-conscious need. The carrying device, and the experts agreed it was a superb one, was the song 'Ballad of Davy Crockett', which was repeated in some form in every Disney show. Also it was richer in symbols than many of the fads: coonskin cap, fringed buckskin, flintlock rifle. TIDE explained: 'All popular movements from Christianity's cross to the Nazi's swastika have their distinctive symbols.'

As for filling a subconscious need, Dr. Dichter had this to say of Crockett: 'Children are reaching for an opportunity to explain themselves in terms of the traditions of the country. Crockett gave them that opportunity. On a very imaginative level the kids really felt they were Davy Crockett ...'

What causes the quick downfall of crazes? The experts said over-exploitation was one cause. Another cause was sociological. Mr. Politz pointed out that crazes take a course from upper to lower. In the case of adult fads this means upper-income education groups to lower. In the case of children, Politz explained: 'Those children who are leaders because of their age adopt the fad first and then see it picked up by the younger children, an age class they no longer wish to be identified with. This causes the older children deliberately to drop the fad.'

These passages also come from Vance Packard but in a book called THE STATUS SEEKERS (1959):

The home during the late fifties began showing signs of supplanting the automobile as the status symbol most favoured by Americans for staking their status claims. There are a number of explanations for this change, but the most important one, undoubtedly, is that with the general rise of incomes and instalment, buying a luxuriously sculptured chariot has become too easily obtainable for the great multitude of status strivers. A home costs more money, a lot more. Another explanation is the appearance in profusion of mass merchandisers in the home-selling field, who have become skilled – partly by copying mass-selling strategies developed in the automobile field – in surrounding their product with status meanings.

While observing the 1958 convention of the nation's home builders in Chicago, I heard one of the featured speakers, a home-marketing consultant, report that he and his aides had conducted 411 'depth interviews' in eight cities to find what people are seeking when they buy a home. In many cases, he reported, mid-century home buyers are buying themselves a symbol of success; and he discussed at length strategies for giving a house being offered for sale 'snob appeal'.

One strategy, he said, is to drop some French phrases into your advertisements. French, he explained, is the language of the snob. Later in the year, we began seeing newspaper advertisements of housing developers drenched in French. One, penned by a developer in Manetto Hills, Long Island, exclaimed: 'C'est Magnifique! Une maison Ranch très originale avec 8 rooms, $2\frac{1}{2}$ baths ... 2-Cadillac garage ... $21,990.'

Some builders began referring to their fifteen by eighteen foot living room as 'The Living Forum' or the 'Reception Galleria', and to their nine by fourteen foot bedroom as 'The Sleeping Chamber'. A split-level house on Long Island became a 'Georgian split, with a bi-level brunch bar in a maitre d'kitchen' and tiny parcels of ground became 'Huge third-acre Estate Sites'. According to one rule-of-thumb, cited by a building consultant, any lot larger than a quarter acre can reasonably be described as an 'estate', and anything larger than half an acre can be labelled as a 'farm'.

... Advertisers are also enthusiastic champions of the Negro's right to consume the good things of American life. Negroes – as they have acquired skills and buying power – have become a $15,000,000,000 market. (The average Negro family reportedly buys twice as much liquor as the average white family.) Also, Negroes are particularly responsive to advertising appeals stressing status because we have forced them to be so preoccupied with status. Their publications take pride in reporting Negro millionaires who ride in Cadillacs; and the publications make the point that 'no self-respecting Negro would smoke a cheap cigarette'.

... With 50,000,000 cars on the road, the challenge was to make car owners by the millions desire to turn in the models they presently owned. The cars became still longer and more expensive-looking. The status meanings of this were brought insistently to the public's attention.

Plymouth quoted a happy family, standing before their long-long car, as disclosing proudly, 'We're not wealthy ... we just look it!' Dodge, in one of its radio commercials, depicted an admiring man exclaiming excitedly to a Dodge owner: 'Boy, you must be rich to own a car as big as this!' In another commercial a wife was angry because her husband was making her wade a long distance through six inches of snow to reach the country-club door. He explained that he didn't want to drive up to the door in their 'little car', and that they couldn't afford a big car. She retorted that they could, if they bought the new sweptwing Dodge.

P12

Can you think of any modern-day crazes which have developed in the same way as the Davy Crockett one?

Think, for example, of all the sales commodities associated with a successful film. You may be able to collect newspaper or magazine articles which help you to trace the progress of a craze.

P13

Have you come across any examples of advertisements which appeal to status-seeking, or which take advantage of children?

P14

What do you think the following advertisements are appealing to? A human weakness? Which? A social class? One particular age group? Are they successful? Do they tell you what you want to know about a product? When you've made up your minds about them, discuss how cleverly the illustrations or language in them are used.

FITLINE — THE FUN WAY TO FITNESS

JUST A FEW MINUTES A DAY JUMPING WITH FITLINE JUMP ROPE
IS THE FUN NEW WAY TO A FITTER TRIMMER BODY.

- FITLINE will improve your all round fitness – which means more vitality, stamina and more energy.
- FITLINE is the easy way to exercise all of the body AT THE SAME TIME in just a few minutes a day, indoors or out.
- FITLINE compares favourably to other forms of exercise, but with Fitline you don't need fine weather or a partner or even a lot of space. It's so compact you can take it with you everywhere.
- FITLINE jump rope has been specially developed as a cheap and very effective way of getting fit and staying fit. Fitline is an indestructable nylon rope. A Patented design perfectly weighted for balance with coloured Polythene handles and sleeves so the rope cannot twist or tangle. No ball-bearings to seize-up or get rusty.
- FITLINE is adjustable to any length for adult or child.

Following the Fitline programme will help develop co-ordination, stamina and tone.

FITLINE — the fun new way to fitness and health for all the family.

ONLY £2.95 inclusive of post and packing. Complete with instructions and fitness programme.

Make the moment last with Fry's Chocolate Cream.

Club Amontillado

Full membership   Waiting list

A CLASSIC MEDIUM DRY SHERRY WITH A SUBTLE NUTTY TASTE. TRY IT CHILLED.

P15

Try designing your own advertisements. You can paint them or act them out as for TV or put them on tape as for radio. But remember that it would be a good idea to decide on an image – a conscious line of approach. The questions in P14 may help you to decide on this.

P16

Some of the following advertising techniques are banned by law or by certain ruling bodies.

In a group, discuss the reasons for banning any or all of them.

    a) Sky-writing or acroplanes carrying banners
    b) periodic, subconsciously-received messages flashed on to the TV
    c) underwear ads wherever children can see them
    d) large trade names on the kit of footballers
    e) sending un-ordered goods through the post and expecting payment
    f) loudspeaker vans

g) cigarettes on TV
h) handbills left under the windscreen wipers of cars
i) door-to-door brush selling
j) neon lights on the motorway.

P17 Divide into groups. The groups will be rival publicity companies hoping to be employed by a firm which has a new product to sell. Decide on the type of product yourself (for example: lipstick, coffee). You have unlimited money to help you start a nationwide advertising and promotion campaign. Think of all the different and most effective methods of advertising; the most imaginative committee will win the firm's contract.

P18 Consider the following statement by Vance Packard:

'The most serious offence many of the depth manipulators (advertisers) commit, it seems to me, is that they try to invade the privacy of our minds. It is the right to privacy in our minds – privacy to be either rational or irrational – that I believe we must strive to protect.'

Arrange a debate and argue one of the following motions:

a) Advertising is an insult to the intelligence.
b) Advertising is an unwelcome intrusion on one's privacy.
c) Advertising makes the world go round.
d) Any publicity is good publicity.

P19 When you worked on P15, did any of you think of using sports or sportsmen and women to advertise? Many people do. Note the following cricket competitions:

a) the Benson & Hedges Cup
b) the John Player League
c) the Prudential Matches
d) the Cornhill Tests.

What do the firms and the sports gain from these sponsorship arrangements?

It is said that a top skier can earn one million pounds per year in payment for using the equipment of a sports firm to whom he or she is contracted.

Top tennis players have agents who negotiate the best terms with sportswear firms – the tennis players will always wear Supersweat headbands, Blanco shorts and use Thunderstreak racquets etc. One famous tennis player shaved off his beard after winning Wimbledon – all the photographs of this momentous event were carefully taken in front of a large advertisement for a certain firm's razor blades.

Look at any football ground. Advertising hoardings are always positioned along the side of the pitch facing TV cameras. BBC officials (forbidden to advertise) used to cover them up before a televised match.

At present, soccer players are not allowed to advertise brand names on their kit unless the label size is strictly controlled. Can you see any objections to these techniques? Or are there only advantages to be had?

SPECIAL NOTE:
In your discussions and debates, no-one should overlook the tremendous amount of good done in sport by firms who advertise by sponsorship. Many top sports competitions would, under present circumstances, not survive were it not for the money provided by such firms. Their motives often seem to be tempered by goodwill.

For example, a sponsoring firm has encouraged fast, free play, together with fairness and good behaviour, by making certain Rugby Union teams this offer: that a sum of money is presented to 'the team of the month' which scores the most tries in that period provided no player is sent off.

Perhaps you can give this some thought and suggest how the idea can be expanded. In football, for example? Could the sponsorship come from the government rather than private firms?

Explore the possibilities in a discussion or essay.

Getting a job

P21

THE YOUTH CAREERS OFFICER

OFFICER: Now look, lad. I'm here to help. To serve the
public. I'm here to find youths careers. That's why I'm
called Youth Careers Officer. I took a course in it.
University Sandwich. I was trained in social psychology.
I was trained in adolescent problems. So now, button your
lip, this is my cubicle. Now, you want a job. What
certificates you got?

HARRY: Certificates?

OFFICER: Mental certificates lad. Exams. GCE, CSE, DD.
Certificates. Qualifications.

HARRY: I've got me Bronze Medallion for Life Saving and
me Tenderfoot in the Cubs.

OFFICER: Is that all?

HARRY: Yes.

OFFICER: So, all we need is a job in a forest, by a lake,
saving lives. Did you get anything else?

HARRY: No.

OFFICER: What, did they not give you anything when
you left?

HARRY: I was supposed to hand me PE kit in, but I
kept it.

The human end of a mechanised system . . .

OFFICER: And that is the sum total of your academic career?

HARRY: Yes.

OFFICER: Well, we could put you to an apprenticeship, on the buildings or in a factory.

HARRY: Apprenticeship is no use. Takes you five years to learn what you could pick up in six months.

OFFICER: You don't want an apprenticeship.

HARRY: No, but I want Saturday afternoons off.

OFFICER: That leaves you with labouring, or semi-skilled.

HARRY: I don't want that.

OFFICER: What sort of thing would you like? Now think about it. I can wait. Take your time. I'm patient. I was trained in psychology and all the rest of it. What sort of job would you like?

HARRY: I would like a job with adventure. Like on the telly. Lots of thrills. Pioneering, life. Colour. Like the pictures. I was brought up on the pictures.

OFFICER: Would you like to try the Police, you've got the height?

HARRY: I don't like law and order. It usually picks on

me. If anything, I would be a cat burglar. But I'm frightened of heights. I keep planning daring daylight robberies but when I get to the stage for shinning up the drainpipe, I can't do it.

OFFICER: Well, all we need to find you is a cat burgling job. Ground floors only. Now come on, come on. I may have done psychology, but I'm not Job. It'll have to be the last stage of a conveyor belt. You can be the human end of a mechanised system, how will that suit you?

from ZIGGER ZAGGER by Peter Terson

P22

One of the most important acts of persuasion you will ever make will be in persuading an employer to give you a job. In this case, of course, it would be unwise to use the wrong method of persuasion. It's no use hanging on to the employer's trouser leg begging and weeping for his favour. Nor is it a good idea to try the aggressive, bullying approach.

The best solution is to show self-respect **and** respect for the person who might be paying your wages for a long time to come.

P23

You're not going to get advice on how to choose a job here. If you need help, and you probably will, you should be able to get it from a local or school Careers Service. Do you know what job you want when you leave school? Don't make the same mistake as Harry in the above extract but don't worry if you haven't made up your mind yet. Just choose a job that you **might** be interested in.

Now write down the name of this job and, underneath, write answers to the following questions about it:

a)   Who would be your employer?
b)   What qualifications would you need?
c)   What experience which you have had would help you to do the job well?
d)   What personal qualities would help you in the job?

P24

How thorough are your answers? Compare them with this purely imaginary example on the facing page:

Job: Gardener
a) Mr. C. Anthemum, proprietor of Chris's Nurseries.
b) CSEs or O levels in English, Maths, Biology.
c) Have helped in school garden for two years.
   Have cultivated family garden for five years.
   Have weekend job gardening for a neighbour.
d) Organised mind, sensitive hands, careful and painstaking.
   Love outdoor work.

P25

Working with a group or the whole class, compile similar lists for the following jobs:

   bus driver, hairdresser,
   architect, mechanic.

P26

So far, the point of what you have done is to get you thinking about **what is required** in every job. Once you know that, you will be able to choose the details about yourself which fit these requirements. Once you have chosen your 'target' and decided how you are suited to it, you can begin the process of persuasion. We can divide that process into two; writing the letter of application and attending an interview.

The letter

P27

Imagine that you wish to apply for one of the jobs advertised here. Write a letter asking for the job.

General Jobs

● Handy Person required 5 mornings per week for busy private decorating firm. Knowledge of VAT an advantage. Own transport necessary: top salary offered to right applicant. Write to: A. Masters, D. P. Jones Ltd, 26 Brown St, Moston.

● GARAGE MECHANIC RE-QUIRED. Young, enthusiastic mechanic wanted to learn trade. Must love engines. Modest pay at first but good prospects. Write to: Mr Miles, Swan Garage, East St, Weston, Blogshire.

Waiter/Waitress wanted. To work in busy hotel during tourist season. Long hours, good pay, accommodation provided. Write to: Mrs Chambers, Bent Elbow Hotel, Stoney Rd, Weston, Blogshire.

P28

Now you've finished the letter, have a good look at it. Compare your effort with those of other people in the class. Which letter is likely to impress the most? Criticise your own letter with these points in mind:

a) Have you set out the letter in the correct way?
b) Is your handwriting neat?
c) How good is the spelling and punctuation?
d) Have you mentioned all the relevant experience, qualities and qualifications you have?
e) Have you been polite?

Be honest, which of these two letters does your version most resemble?

3, Lodge Lane,
Crankstone.

Dear Secretary,
          I would like the job as steward at the British Legion as I am quite interested in being a waiter. I have two O levels, could you tell me what the pay is.

K.E. Hurst.

3, Lodge Lane,
Crankstone,
Sussex
7. 7. 78

Dear Sir,

I am writing in answer to your advertisement in the Evening Standard on the seventh of this month. I would like very much to apply for the post of steward as I am about to leave school in two weeks time.

I have recently sat O level examinations in English Language and Mathematics and await the results. I believe myself to be good with figures, polite and personable. I have had two years of experience in a part time post as waiter in a local hotel and the proprietor would be glad to provide a reference if required. I would be very happy to attend an interview at your convenience.

Yours faithfully,
KE Hurst

Neither of these examples is perfect but one is noticeably better than the other. It follows the rules of layout. (Notice the positioning of address, date, first two lines and last two lines of the letter.)

The second letter is reasonably neat. It is polite. It is literate! It includes the information which may help a possible employer to decide whether to interview the writer.

Did you think about all these things before you wrote your letter?

P30 In groups, imagine you are employers in a firm. Decide on three or four jobs you can offer and write out advertisements for them. Decide very clearly on what kind of person you want to employ, what qualifications and qualities are needed.

P31 Pass your advertisements on to another group and take theirs in return. Now you are looking for a job and get another chance – write a better application for one of the jobs this time. When everyone has finished, swap letters with the other group and write short notes of criticism on each. Which of the applicants would you interview?

P32 None of this may seem like persuasion but, of course, it is. You are persuading someone to become attracted to you by what you say and do. At the interview, this becomes even more important. Before we study this, discuss the way you think people should dress and behave at an interview.

The interview

P33 Some of you may well consider school uniforms to be pointless and something of a burden. But have you ever stopped to consider how many other groups of people have to wear a uniform of a kind? Not only policemen, firemen and traffic wardens, but practically everyone; teachers, shop assistants, housewives, bank clerks and so on. You can prove this by describing how you expect each of these examples to dress.

P34 Rightly or wrongly, the majority of employers believe in these expectations of dress. Look at this newspaper article and discuss the views expressed in it:

Here's why you may be jobless

If you want to get ahead GET SMART

PAUL LOFTHOUSE is wearing a suit, white shirt and tie bought for a total of £59 in the sales at Peter Brown of Oxford St., London.

Lyn Mitchell's hacking jacket cost £28, her matching culottes £18.95 and her silk blouse £11.50. All supplied by Fenwicks of Bond Street.

YOU'VE JUST left school with the right qualifications. You're getting lots of interviews . . . but somehow you're never the one who gets the job. So what's wrong?

Examine Paul Lofthouse and model Lyn Mitchell in the picture then take a look at yourself. If you dress like them, **THAT'S WHAT'S WRONG.**

For even in these days of doing your own thing in jeans and T-shirts, most employers still insist on youngsters doing **THEIR** thing during office hours.

And that means smartening up, just like Paul and Lyn have done in the picture on the right.

Like it or not, that was the hard news yesterday from Richard O'Brien, chairman of the Manpower Services Commission.

Speaking at a conference in London, he revealed that next to faults in personality and attitude, appearance and manners were the biggest reason why young people were turned down for jobs.

Employers still want decently turned-out young recruits who will give outsiders a good impression of the company, said Mr. O'Brien.

Story: CHARLES LYTE

Pictures: KENT GAVIN

The importance of a clean, neat appearance is something the giant ICI firm has known for a long time, however.

It is running a special course in the North East in which school-leavers learn the 'dos' and 'don'ts' of interviews.

A company spokesman said: 'If youngsters don't take a pride in themselves they are not going to take a pride in the job . . .'

Schools should do more to help youngsters avoid the pitfalls of job interviews. 'At the moment, teachers do not know how industry works,' the spokesman added.

Impressed

I asked other firms: Is dressing smartly really THAT important for a young job-hunter?

A major employer of secretarial staff said: 'When applicants come to interviews we expect them to be neatly dressed and clean, not wearing jeans.

'We look for clean hair, tidy dress, and moderate make-up—and we are impressed by a skirt and blouse or a dress.'

An international chain store said it wouldn't worry if management job-seekers turn up in jeans—'We know they would turn up for work in a suit.'

But for countersales staff, it would expect interviewees to be 'neatly presented and well turned out.'

But one of Britain's biggest engineering companies doesn't worry about appearances.

A spokesman said: 'If youngsters have the right educational requirements and are motivated in the right way they will get the job—even if they are scruffy.'

But how can we? ask the kids

YOUNGSTERS interviewed around Britain yesterday had a straight answer to the advice that they should dress more smartly.

We just cannot afford to, they said.

Unemployed waitress Anne Lacey, 18, said in Bristol: 'It is not easy to be smart if you are on the dole.'

'It is a vicious circle. Without good clothes you can't get a job—without a job you can't afford new clothes.' But others thought it was good advice—and said they followed it.

Mickey O'Connor, 16, who works in a London insurance office canteen, said: 'I got the job because I looked smart, have short hair and can give a bit of chat.

'Blimey, I looked like an MP, compared with some of the applicants.'

Susan Javes, 16, of Wideopen, Northumberland, said girls should dress up for interviews.

'A girl should dress like a girl—no matter what the women's libbers say,' she said, 'that means a smart dress, shoes and nylons.

'Girls spoil their chances by wearing jeans. I know one girl who went to an interview dressed in a cat suit. She didn't get the job.'

Boots

Jimmy Bowen, 16, from Bristol, lost a job as a porter at a hotel because another boy had a smarter pair of trousers.

'The manager said I should wear better trousers, but my jeans were clean and well-pressed,' Jimmy said.

Londoner, Wayne Barry, 16, said: 'I do not think it matters how you dress for an interview. I went for my job as a messenger in jeans, boots and a 'T'-shirt.

'But a mate of mine who dresses smartly and has 'O'-levels, can't get work because he's after something at a higher level.

'That's the problem—there just aren't any jobs around. You have to grab what you can and hang on.'

In Newcastle, Geoff Graham, 16, who has been looking for a job as a painter for four months, said:

'If I go to an interview I always wear a tie, shirt and jacket. The night before I wash my hair and clean my shoes. Nobody told me to do that. It's just commonsense.'

Snakes

But he still does not have a job.

Steven Staple, 17, from Battersea, who was working on a Government job creation scheme, yesterday, said: 'The real problem is that the jobs aren't there.'

He has snakes tattooed on his arms and yesterday he wore a silver razor blade on a chain around his neck.

'I don't think I've ever been turned down for a job because of the way I look,' he said.

'But any kid who goes for a job dressed as a punk rocker would be stupid.'

Tattooes did not help Lea Higginbottom, 17, of Manchester, who left school with three CSEs and one O-level.

He said: 'I have been trying to get work now for eight months.

'When I went for one job the manager looked at all the tattoos on my arms and asked me why i had them. I didn't get the job.'

Wendy Humphreys, an art student from Manchester, said: 'I would wear smart clothes for an interview if I thought the firm would mind.

'But why can't managers just accept people as they are?'

P35

It is evident that some employers are persuaded by dress and many, believe it or not, are also persuaded by the way you look, move or talk.

Split into pairs. One partner will be an employer waiting in an office, the other will be the person to be interviewed, the applicant. In the 'office' go through the motions of meeting each other to begin the interview.

P36

Now look carefully at how some of the pairs dealt with this seemingly simple task. Perhaps some applicants scuttle in like nervous rabbits; others may tower over an employer with a threatening look.

P37

Before you continue with your practice interview, consider how you might prepare for it. The following points may be helpful to you:

a) Discuss the job with your parents beforehand – especially if you aim to take it before you are eighteen.
b) Think of some of the questions you may be asked at the interview. About your studies, your interests and your ambitions, perhaps. Can you answer them in a complete and interesting way?
c) Think of some questions **you** can ask about the job. You will have to know about conditions, pay, hours, prospects and other details but **don't** go leaping in with questions about holidays, teabreaks and rest periods – your main priority. Try to show an interest in the work, not just your time off.

P38

Using the material and ideas you created in P30, P31 and P32, it might now be possible to set up mock interviews in which the employers meet the applicants.

Make sure that employers and applicants are well prepared with facts, ideas and questions before the interviews start. Remember, too, that the main value of this exercise will be involved in accepting friendly criticism from each other.

ARGUMENT

Clouding the issue

When you listen to, or read, someone else's argument, you should be aware of how logical the argument is. You should also look out for certain tricks which are included, purposely or not, to obscure the truth and influence your mind falsely. This subsection is concerned with some of them.

Lies, damned lies and statistics

A1

In order to prove their point, many people will use the evidence of statistics – lists of figures which are intended to point something out about the subject. Yet they are not always what they seem. Look at this example of the misuse of statistics:

In the town of Little Doing, unemployment figures for 1970 were 300 and, for 1975, 400. Therefore, it can be said that unemployment has increased by thirty-three per cent in five years.

Or can it?

The figures don't include the fact that the working-age population increased from 600 to 800 in those five years. If you can do your sums quickly, you will see that the percentage of people unemployed has stayed the same!

Therefore the figures cannot be used to show that unemployment is increasing – can they?

Statistics are often carefully selected in this way and you may need more information before you can judge the conclusions that some people might draw from them.

A2

Study these statistics and answer the questions which follow:

A STUDY OF LEISURE TIME AS USED BY THE FIFTH YEAR OF BLOGSHIRE HIGH SCHOOL
Number in year = 100
Number who finished reading a novel in the last week = 15
Number who watched over 16 hours of television
                                in the last week = 60
Number who went to a disco in the last week   = 25
Number who spent more than 5 hours on a hobby
                                in the last week = 30

a) Can you draw any conclusions from these figures?
b) Can they be used to 'prove' anything?
c) Could they be used to 'prove' anything if more information were available?
d) Are these statements proved by the figures?
  'People in the fifth year spend more time watching television than reading.'
  'Seventy per cent of the fifth year don't have a hobby.'
e) How would you carry out a survey to draw conclusions about use of leisure time among the members of your form? What questions would you ask? Try carrying out such a survey.

Prejudice

Study these arguments very carefully and attempt to say whether they are reasonable or based on prejudice:

a) Publican: 'I refuse to serve young girls who drink out of pint glasses. It is unladylike.'
b) Teacher: 'I never give good marks to someone who does not take care to write neatly. It is a sign of disrespect.'
c) Householder: 'I wouldn't like to live in the same street as coloured people. I am not a racialist but the price of the property would stay low if I wanted to sell.'
d) Parent: 'I would not like my children to go to a comprehensive school. It would turn them into hooligans.'
e) Teenager: 'I never read any of the books my father recommends. They are bound to be boring if adults like them.'

You may share the prejudices of someone who is using them to argue a point, but that doesn't mean that the argument is therefore valid.

Write an essay about one particular prejudice which you object to.

False logic

What is wrong with this sequence of statements?

> Hunting is cruel.
> Hunting is an upper class sport.
> Therefore the upper classes are cruel.

Do they follow logically or is there an error somewhere?
Don't be misled by such statements.
Read the following and decide which are logical:

    a) I am an Englishman.
       I like dogs.
       Therefore all Englishmen like dogs.
    b) Cars have four wheels.
       Cars are motor vehicles.
       Therefore all motor vehicles have four wheels.
    c) Women have long hair.
       Women are different from men.
       Therefore men do not have long hair.
    d) I am whistling.
       Nervous people whistle.
       Therefore I am nervous.

See if you can invent similar three-line statements about the
following and then analyse them closely:
    a) women drivers
    b) school dinners
    c) policemen.

Cliché and jargon

What is a cliché and what is jargon? Look up the words
in a dictionary. Some examples are used for 'padding' an
argument when a shorter or better phrase would do just
as well. Look at these examples (often used in speeches or
arguments) and try to say what is wrong with them and
how you would replace them:

> 'At this moment in time ...'
> 'The fact of the matter is ...'
> 'This has the effect of ...'

Most of these are just harmless waffle and often make a statement sound more important than it really is. Put this short paragraph into simple and understandable language:

> Following consultation with the principal of this educational establishment concerning my non-functioning with regard to the academic timetable, it has been decided that I be placed in a punishment-situation forthwith and without further delay.

Write a short piece arguing the case for not doing homework using this type of pompous language.

Some clichés are more harmful when they give a false impression of the facts.
'Long haired layabouts' suggests that all people with long hair are lazy.
'Football hooligans' suggests that all football fans are violent.
'Trade union troublemakers' also links two sets of people as though they automatically belong together. Can you think of any other cliché terms of abuse which are in common use?
If your arguments are to be well-reasoned, you must avoid using such terms.

Rhetoric and oratory

Some people are gifted with the ability to speak inspiringly and stirringly in front of a crowd of people. It is a pleasurable and exciting experience to listen to such a person but it is also a dangerous one. Logical and rational argument can be forgotten as the speaker drives his points home, often using the kind of inaccurate clichés mentioned above. An emotional crowd can be used, in this way, to behave as a speaker wants them to without rational thought. This was one of the skills which made Hitler, for example, such a successful leader.

> Hitler always showed a distrust of argument and criticism. Unable to argue coolly himself, since his early days in Vienna his one resort had been to shout his opponent down. The questioning of his assumptions or his facts rattled him and threw him out of his stride, less because of any intellectual

inferiority than because words, and even facts, were to him not a means of rational communication and logical analysis, but devices for manipulating emotion. The introduction of intellectual processes of criticism and analysis marked the intrusion of hostile elements which disturbed the exercise of this power. Hence Hitler's hatred of the intellectual: in the masses, 'instinct is supreme and from instinct comes faith ... While the healthy common folk instinctively close their ranks to form a community of the people, the intellectuals run this way and that, like hens in a poultry yard. With them it is impossible to make history; they cannot be used as elements supporting a community.'

For the same reason Hitler rated the spoken above the written word: 'False ideas and ignorance may be set aside by means of instruction, but emotional resistance never can. Nothing but an appeal to hidden forces will be effective here. And that appeal can scarcely be made by any writer. Only the orator can hope to make it.'

As an orator Hitler had obvious faults. The timbre of his voice was harsh, very different from the beautiful quality of Goebbels'. He spoke at too great length; was often repetitive and verbose; lacked lucidity and frequently lost himself in cloudy phrases. These short-comings, however, mattered little beside the extraordinary impression of force, the immediacy of passion, the intensity of hatred, fury, and menace conveyed by the sound of the voice alone without regard to what he said.

One of the secrets of his mastery over a great audience was his instinctive sensitivity to the mood of a crowd, a flair for divining the hidden passions, resentments and longings in their minds. In MEIN KAMPF he says of the orator: 'He will always follow the lead of the great mass in such a way that from the living emotion of his hearers the apt word which he needs will be suggested to him and in its turn this will go straight to the hearts of his hearers.'

One of his most bitter critics, Otto Strasser, wrote: 'Hitler responds to the vibration of the human heart with the delicacy of a seismograph, or perhaps of a wireless receiving set, enabling him, with a certainty with which no conscious gift could endow him, to act as a loudspeaker proclaiming the most secret desires, the least admissible instincts, the sufferings, and personal revolts of a whole nation.... I have been asked many times what is the secret of Hitler's extraordinary power as a speaker. I can only attribute it to his uncanny intuition, which infallibly diagnoses the ills from which his audience is suffering. If he tries to bolster up his argument with theories or quotations from books he has only imperfectly understood, he scarcely rises above a very poor mediocrity. But let him throw away his crutches and step out boldly, speaking as the spirit moves him, and he is promptly transformed into one of the greatest speakers of the century. Adolf enters a hall. He sniffs the air. For a minute he gropes, feels his way, senses the atmosphere. Suddenly he bursts forth. His words go like an arrow to their target, he touches each private wound on the raw, liberating the mass unconscious expressing its innermost aspirations, telling it what it most wants to hear.'

Hitler's power to bewitch an audience has been likened to the occult arts of the African medicine-man or the Asiatic Shaman; others have compared it to the sensitivity of a medium, and the magnetism of a hypnotist.

from HITLER by Alan Bullock

And Hitler proceeded to make his audience, which con-
sisted mostly of women nurses and social workers, laugh – and
then applaud hysterically. He was faced with the problem
of answering two questions uppermost in the minds of the
German people: When would Britain be invaded, and what
would be done about the night bombings of Berlin and other
German cities? As to the first:

'In England they're filled with curiosity and keep asking,
"Why doesn't he come?" Be calm. Be calm. He's coming!
He's coming!'

His listeners found that crack very funny, but they also
believed that it was an unequivocal pledge. As to the bombings, he began by a typical falsification and ended with a
dire threat:

'Just now ... Mr Churchill is demonstrating his new brain
child, the night air raid. Mr Churchill is carrying out these
raids not because they promise to be highly effective, but
because his Air Force cannot fly over Germany in daylight
... whereas German planes are over English soil every
day ... Whenever the Englishman sees a light, he drops a
bomb ... on residential districts, farms and villages.'

And then came the threat.

'For three months I did not answer because I believed
that such madness would be stopped. Mr Churchill took
this for a sign of weakness. We are now answering night
for night.

When the British Air Force drops two or three or four
thousand kilograms of bombs, then we will in one night
drop 150–, 230–, 300– or 400,000 kilograms.'

At this point, according to my diary, Hitler had to pause
because of the hysterical applause of the German women
listeners.

'When they declare', Hitler continued, 'that they will increase their attacks on our cities, then we will **raze** their
cities to the ground.' At this, I noted, the young ladies were
quite beside themselves and applauded phrenetically. When
they had recovered, he added, 'We will stop the handiwork
of these night air pirates, so help us God!'

On hearing this, I also noted, 'The young German women
hopped to their feet and, their breasts heaving, screamed their
approval!'

'The hour will come,' Hitler concluded, 'when one of
us will break, and it will not be National Socialist Germany'.
At this, I finally noted, 'The raving maidens kept their heads

sufficiently to break their wild shouts of joy with a chorus of "Never! Never!" '

from THE RISE AND FALL OF THE THIRD REICH
by William Shirer

a) Have you ever been part of a group or crowd which has got 'carried away'? Did you find yourself doing things that you didn't really want to?

b) At trade union meetings, votes are often taken by a show of hands after speeches have been given. Discuss the advantages and disadvantages of this method when compared to a secret ballot.

Show of hands at a Trade Union meeting.

c) Read the speeches of Napoleon and Squealer in ANIMAL
    FARM by George Orwell. They convince listeners that
    what **seems** to be true is, in reality, not true. In doing
    so, Napoleon and Squealer are taking advantage of
    people's naivety – telling lies which seem to be true.
    In order to see how this technique works, put yourself
    in the position of a ruler who has just banned public
    meetings of more than three people and imposed a
    curfew which restricts people's movements. These
    moves are really intended to keep the ruler safe from
    rebellion, but how would you convince the people that
    they are really for their own good?

Patriotism

A7

Before reading the passages which follow, consider your
views on patriotism. These questions may guide your
thoughts:

a) What groups do you belong to – starting with
    your family and moving outwards?
b) Is it important to belong to these groups? Which
    do you feel most strongly attached to?
c) Would you defend any of these groups if they
    were threatened in some way?
d) Do you feel antagonistic or contemptuous to-
    wards other groups, for example: foreigners,
    other football supporters, 'snobs'? Be honest.
e) Do you support your country's sports teams and
    care whether they win or lose?
f) Would you fight for your country? Even if you
    thought it was in the wrong?

A8

Write an essay defending or attacking your (or someone
else's) allegiance to a club, group or gang.

A9

Study the following passages and posters and write an
essay arguing your views on one of the following:

Patriotism is the last refuge of a scoundrel.
It is sweet and fitting to die for one's country.
Is war ever justified?

I vow to thee, my country – all earthly things above –
Entire and whole and perfect, the service of my love,
The love that asks no questions: the love that stands the test,
That lays upon the altar the dearest and the best:
The love that never falters, the love that pays the price,
The love that makes undaunted the final sacrifice.

from I VOW TO THEE, MY COUNTRY by Sir Cecil Spring-Rice

WHY PATRIOTS ARE A BIT NUTS IN THE HEAD

Patriots are a bit nuts in the head
because they wear
red, white and blue-
tinted spectacles
(red for blood
white for glory
and blue ...
for a boy)
and are in effervescent danger
of losing their lives
lives are good for you
when you are alive
you can eat and drink a lot
and go out with girls
(sometimes if you are lucky
*   you can even go to bed with them)*
but you can't do this
if you have your belly shot away
and your seeds

spread over some corner of a foreign field
to facilitate
in later years
the growing of oats by some peasant yobbo
when you are posthumous it is cold and dark
and that is why patriots are a bit nuts in the head.

Roger McGough

I am always amazed when I hear people saying that sport creates goodwill between the nations, and that if only the common peoples of the world could meet one another at football or cricket, they would have no inclination to meet on the battlefield. Even if one didn't know from concrete examples (the 1936 Olympic Games, for instance) that international sporting contests lead to orgies of hatred, one could deduce it from general principles.

Nearly all the sports practised nowadays are competitive. You play to win, and the game has little meaning unless you do your utmost to win. On the village green, where you pick up sides and no feeling of local patriotism is involved, it is possible to play simply for the fun and exercise: but as soon as the question of prestige arises, as soon as you feel that you and some larger unit will be disgraced if you lose, the most savage combative instincts are aroused. Anyone who has played even in a school football match knows this. At the international level sport is frankly mimic warfare. But the significant thing is not the behaviour of the players

but the attitude of the spectators: and, behind the spectators, of the nations who work themselves into furies over these absurd contests, and seriously believe – at any rate for short periods – that running, jumping and kicking a ball are tests of national virtue....

If you wanted to add to the vast fund of ill-will existing in the world at this moment, you could hardly do it better than by a series of football matches between Jews and Arabs, Germans and Czechs, Indians and British, Russians and Poles, and Italians and Yugoslavs, each match to be watched by a massed audience of 100,000 spectators. I do not, of course, suggest that sport is one of the main causes of international rivalry; big-scale sport is itself, I think, merely another effect of the causes that have produced nationalism. Still, you do make things worse by sending forth a team of eleven men, labelled as national champions, to do battle against some rival team, and allowing it to be felt on all sides that whichever nation is defeated will 'lose face'.

from THE SPORTING SPIRIT by George Orwell (1945)

HELLO HANS

Written after visiting the German War Graves Cemetery at Cannock Chase.

Well, hello Hans,
I was passing so I stopped to say hello.
You don't know me and there's no reason why you should ever
*   know.*
You died here, in some prison camp, conditions weren't so bad,
Was it a wound, Hans, or maybe the shellshock sent you mad?
You were twenty, that's what it says upon the stone.
I'm trying to imagine what it's like to die all alone,
At twenty, before you've had a chance to be outgrown.
I was passing so I stopped to say hello.

Did you see the child, Hans?
The little girl who danced upon your grave.
Not yours, Hans, not the ones you went to war to save.
See her father, he proudly picks her up and sets her down,
On a tombstone to take photographs that he can show around.
He was a young boy at the very moment that you died.
Maybe you had a little child to walk proudly by your side
Or a young wife, who tried so very hard, but still she cried.
Did you see the little girl dance on your grave?

Can you see the lovers, Hans?
Eating their ice cream and holding hands.
You see you're funny, Hans, you're good business for the ice
*   cream vans.*
They moved you here, why I'll never really understand;
This is useless ground, nothing ever grows upon this land.
But the gesture was made, at little cost, no-one would mind,
And the tourists would gaze at any funny thing that they might
*   find;*
And such gestures helped to leave the memories behind.
See the lovers, ever young, holding hands.
Well, goodbye Hans,
I'll maybe come again some other time.
Because somehow, that grave that's yours could easily be mine.
You see there's wars, Hans, men are trained to fight each other
*   still.*
It goes on, Hans, it always has – it seems it always will.
But I must go now, the young men milling round are making
*   so much noise,*
And, as you remember, when they're together boys will always
*   just be boys*
Unlike you, Hans, they've never been a country's broken toys.
So goodbye, I'll maybe come again some other time.

a song by Harvey Andrews

Censorship

A10

Are you fully aware of how much censorship exists in our society? In which areas is censorship practised? For what reason? By whom?

A11

Again, these questions may help you to get your views clear:

  a) Do you feel that, if certain things are not censored, they might corrupt people's minds? What things?
  b) Have you seen examples of such things? If so, have you been corrupted? Do you know anyone who has? Or might be?
  c) What other arguments are there in favour of

censorship? Do you think that everything is permissible and that people should decide for themselves?

Study the following passages and then write an essay of your choice, arguing your views on the subject:

When it comes to the so-called obscene words, I should say that hardly one person in a million escapes mob-reaction. The first reaction is almost sure to be mob-reaction, mob-indignation, mob-condemnation. And the mob gets no further. But the real individual has second thoughts and says: Am I really shocked? Do I really feel outraged and indignant? And the answer of any individual is bound to be: No, I am not shocked, not outraged, nor indignant. I know the word, and take it for what it is, and I am not going to be jockeyed into making a mountain out of a mole-hill, not for all the law in the world.

from PORNOGRAPHY AND OBSCENITY by D. H. Lawrence

Myself, I am mystified at this horror over a mere word, a plain simple word that stands for a plain simple thing. 'In the beginning was the Word, and the Word was God and the Word was with God.'
If that is true, then we are very far from the beginning. When did the Word 'fall'? When did the Word become unclean 'below the navel'? . . . . . Whoever the God was that made us, He made us complete. He didn't stop at the navel and leave the rest to the devil. . . . The word arse is as much good as the word face. It must be so, otherwise you cut off your god at the waist.

from INTRODUCTION TO 'PANSIES' by D. H. Lawrence

Perhaps the best and most readily understood form of 'censorship' today is that ordinance which forbids driving faster than 30 mph in a built-up area. It is an intolerable interference with liberty. Often it appears so unnecessary. Many decent drivers could happily career through the streets of our cities (if traffic conditions permitted) at 60 mph and would rarely, if ever, collide with a lorry or knock down and kill a three-year old child. Everybody **knows** this. Yet the appalling statistics are there. There are lunatics, it appears, who cannot drive to begin with; who get inordinately drunk; who fall asleep at the wheel – who do a myriad things they shouldn't and who end up killing or maiming themselves (which may not be altogether a bad thing) and much worse, clouting some other innocent often fatally.

In a society where violent thuggery has not been eliminated; where robbery, rape, stealing, brutality *ad nauseam* continue to flourish; where millions of pounds are spent on efforts to educate and reform and deter, the idea that **all** forms of censorship should be abandoned may well appear *outré*. It sits with the idea that as the road toll mounts, all speed limits should be abandoned and all penalties for dangerous driving, drunken driving and so on, jettisoned. Some will still drive dangerously, some will still drive drunkenly – the road casualties will mount; but as all this happens, does the argument for abolishing all control thereby lose force?

In a sense this is what censorship is all about. Is it right to call a halt at some point, however far along the road? Or is it better to allow unfettered liberty perhaps leading to a society which can enjoy both liberty **and** death?

from MARY WHITEHOUSE by Max Caulfield

April 4th, 1984. Last night to the flicks. All war films. One very good one of a ship full of refugees being bombed somewhere in the Mediterranean. Audience much amused by shots of a great huge fat man trying to swim away with a helicopter after him, first you saw him wallowing along in the water like a porpoise, then you saw him through the helicopters gunsights, then he was full of holes and the sea round him turned pink and he sank as suddenly as though the holes had let in the water. audience shouting with laughter when he sank. then you saw a lifeboat full of children with a helicopter hovering over it. there was a middle-aged woman might have been a jewess sitting up in the bow with a little boy about three years old in her arms. little boy screaming with fright and hiding his head between her breasts as if he was trying to burrow right into her and the woman putting her arms round him and comforting him although she was blue with fright herself, all the time covering him up as much as possible as if she thought her arms could keep the bullets off him. then the helicopter planted a 20 kilo bomb in among them terrific flash and the boat went all to matchwood. then there was a wonderful shot of a child's arm going up up up right up into the air a helicopter with a camera in its nose must have followed it up and there was a lot of applause from the party seats

but a woman down in the prole part of the house suddenly
started kicking up a fuss and shouting they didnt oughter
of showed it not in front of kids they didnt it aint right
not in front of kids it aint until the police turned her out
i dont suppose anything happened to her nobody cares what
the proles say typical prole reaction they never − −

from 1984 by George Orwell

A13

In 1913, films could be censored for showing the following
things (among others):

- cruelty to animals
- indecorous dancing
- indelicate sexual situations
- gruesome murders
- medical operations
- cruelty to women
- drunken scenes carried to excess
- native customs in foreign lands abhorrent to British
  ideas.
- the materialisation of Christ or the Almighty.

And, in 1925

- irreverent Biblical quotations
- libels on the British nursing profession
- grossly vulgar and offensive travesties of the War
- provocative and sensuous exposure of girls' legs.

In 1966, the Greater London Council said:

No film shall be exhibited ...
a) which is likely −

  i) To encourage or to incite to crime; or
  ii) to lead to disorder; or
  iii) to stir up hatred against any section of the public
       in Great Britain on the grounds of colour, race or
       ethnic or national origins; or

b) the effect of which is, if taken as a whole, such as to
   tend to deprave and corrupt persons who are likely to
   see it.

How have things changed?
Could you compile a list of things which should be censored
in films? Or on TV?

INSTRUCTION

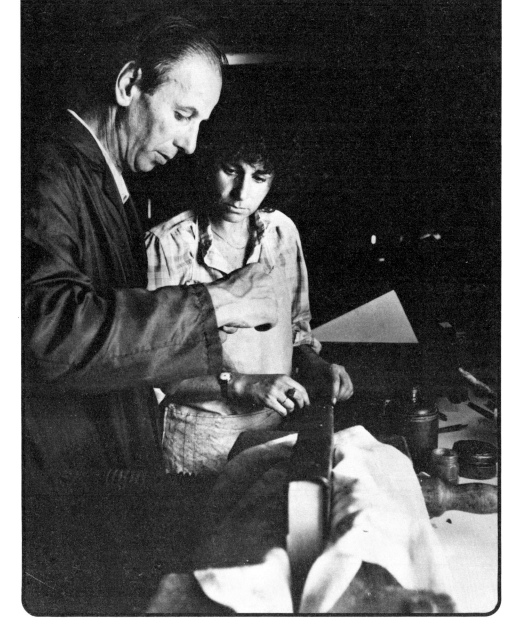

In a sense, this book could be called an 'Instruction Manual'. We are trying to 'instruct' you in how to become a better talker, reader, writer and listener. We do this by suggesting activities which we think will develop further and more widely the language skills you already possess.

These aims are very broad, however. Most instruction manuals confine themselves to a simple definite task: changing spark plugs, making a cabinet, growing peas or cooking a dish.

I1

ROASTED CHICKEN — CHINESE STYLE

I 3–4 lb chicken   I tablespoon soya sauce
½ cup of 'hot' sauce   spring onions cleaned and cut
3 tablespoons orange peel   into 1½ inch pieces
3 teaspoons sugar   sherry

After ensuring that the chicken is completely dry (stand it in a warm oven for a few minutes), it should be rubbed with a marinade composed of the sugar, soya sauce and 'hot' sauce; this should be rubbed well into the meat. The chicken should then be left to stand for two hours, before stuffing with the spring onions and peel. Pour over the rest of the marinade with a little sherry and place in a preheated oven at 350 degrees for 1¼ hours.

  The chicken may then be carved or, preferably, chopped into a number of pieces and served with rice, bean-sprouts, peppers, mushrooms and bamboo shoots.

What do you notice about the type of language used here? What differences are there between this type of prose and that used in a story or a poem? Is the author writing for someone who already knows a little about Chinese cooking (or any kind of cooking), or is he writing for a novice?

Consider your audience

I2

In this section we shall be asking you to devise an 'Instruction Manual' that could be used by others, successfully, for learning.

Some possible subjects:

car maintenance	wine making
'customising' cars	playing chess
cooking Indian food	weaving
goalkeeping	printing
nine pin bowling	playing golf
playing billiards	building and running a disco
oil painting	organizing a successful party
building a wall	modelling.

When writing an instruction manual however, you should consider carefully whom you intend it to be read by. Consider your audience. A 'novice' audience may need a careful explanation of points you think are obvious, a higher proportion of diagrams, the use of short clear sentences, an avoidance of jargon.

13

Below are examples of technical terms from TECHNICAL DRAWING AND ELECTRONICS explained by pupils for 'laymen'. The first two explain an ellipse.

AN ELLIPSE AS A CONIC SECTION
First of all you must think of a cone which is sliced through the centre horizontally, but is slightly slanted. When you look at this circle it seems rather squashed. In fact, it is oval and is called an ellipse.

An ellipse is a squashed circle like an egg. Take a cone, with the closed end uppermost and the wide (closed or open) end resting on the table. If you then cut a slice off the top on the slant the original pointed end will be shaped like an ellipse. It is called a conic section because you have to use a cone to produce it.

Which of these two explanations is the more successful? Write down any words or phrases which show that the writer is 'talking' to a novice audience. What methods can be used to describe shapes **in words**? Write down any examples of phrases that might be useful.

14

In the following passage, the student is attempting to explain what a printed circuit is, and how to make one:

EXPLANATION OF PRINTED CIRCUITS

To have an electric circuit, to make something electrical work, you need a power source, (e.g. a battery), something electrical you want to make work, and some way of connecting the two. In a lot of circuits, (e.g. the wiring of house lights) copper wire which is coated in plastic is used, but in smaller circuits the copper lines are put on to a piece of plastic, and the two objects are attached directly to the plastic and copper. (OK? Got that? If you haven't I shall scream, tear my hair, and start again, but if all is well, let us proceed.)

It is made by painting the pattern of copper you want on to a piece of plastic, which has been coated with copper on one side. You use a special ink to paint with, which resists acid. Then you dump the thing in acid, and wait until the copper which hasn't been painted over is eaten away. When you have removed the ink, you have the basis of a printed circuit, and you only have to attach the power supply and whatever you want to make work at the other end.

Discuss the methods used here by the writer.

I 5

Write an explanation of a technical idea you have learned at school for the benefit of a non-expert. (Your teacher may be an ideal audience!)

I 6

Write down one- or two-sentence explanations for the following mathematical terms:

a) subtract   e) square root
b) even number   f) factor
c) multiply   g) zero
d) divide   h) percentage.

I 7

You probably remember your first day at your present school. Write a clear instruction leaflet entitled: 'How to Survive The First Day At School'.

I 8

Look at some of the textbooks you use at school.
Discuss the type of language used in them. Do they differ? Do some of them 'talk over your head'?

Select the best one. Make brief notes on its method: how

is it organised, what level of vocabulary is used, how are technical terms (jargon) explained?

19

Collect together some Instruction Manuals and leaflets – look for examples of poor instructions as well as the clearer kind, and make notes on method as for 18.

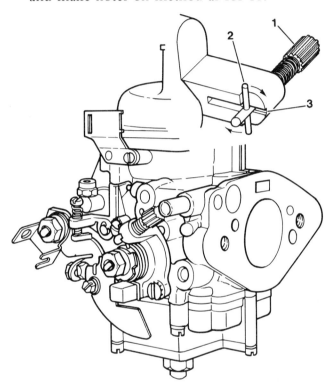

A new owner of a Vauxhall car is provided with an instruction leaflet on basic maintenance. It includes the following:

Carburetter cold start adjustment

The carburetter incorporates a two-position spring-loaded choke stop, which controls the position of the mechanism in the cold start (choke) position. The choke stop has a pin which seats either against a shoulder or in a groove in the mounting. When the stop (1) is set with the pin at right angles to the groove as shown in (2), the travel of the cold start device is restricted to a position which will provide the required enrichment to permit starting down to − 18°C.

Where the ambient temperature regularly falls below

−18°C, the stop (1) should be turned so that the pin engages in the groove as shown at (3), to allow maximum travel of the cold start device.

a) Is the instruction capable of being understood by
   i) someone with no knowledge of cars at all,
   ii) someone with some basic knowledge,
   iii) an expert on cars?
b) Is any vocabulary used which requires explanation?
c) Can the instruction be understood without the diagram?

I 10

Write a short explanation of the method of operating a domestic appliance − such as a washing machine. Include a diagram, if necessary. Exchange your work with a partner. Do you clearly understand what he has written, and vice versa? Do any changes have to be made as a result of this?

I 11

Write a definition of the language term 'sentence' for the benefit of a young child. Can you define 'adjective', 'verb', and 'adverb' in the same way?

I 12

In a small group, set up a 'production-line' making a product such as jam (see Peter Terson's factory scene in ZIGGER ZAGGER). Direct the group members in the mime, each one being a machine in the manufacturing process. Then introduce a new apprentice who has to be taught the job and develop this into a scene.

I 13

The following are instructions to be carried out in a particular type of emergency:

   a) pull faces and gesticulate wildly
   b) fix copper acetate tablets to each leg
   c) shout as loudly as possible
   d) if the above fail, stay close to your partner and watch each other's feet.

In small groups try to decide what these instructions refer to. Then improvise a short scene in which the emergency arises, and you take the actions described above.
(Solution: at the end of the section.)

I 14

Bring a **simple** instruction sheet to school, such as that found with plastic kits, cardboard cut-out models or sewing patterns. Copy the verbal instructions, then delete them from the diagram: hand it to your partner who should then devise suitable instructions. Compare his attempt with the original.

I 15

You will by now have realised the differing roles of words and diagrams in 'instructions'. Having decided on the subject and audience for your Instruction Manual, you should use the knowledge you have gained in organising and presenting your work.

You may like to organise your instruction manual on, for example, growing peas, in the following way:

1   Introduction
2   Types
3   Preparing the soil
4   Seeding
5   Mulching
6   Cultivation: a) staking b) using trellis
7   Controlling Pests
8   Harvesting and storing.

Side-headings and sub-sections, possibly numbered in step-by-step order, will be most useful to you, since you are not writing a lengthy book.

Statistics or technical data can often be presented using a well devised chart, as in this recipe book:

OVEN TEMPERATURES

	Degrees Fahrenheit	Regulo (for gas cookers)	Degrees Centigrade
Very slow	240–80	$\frac{1}{4}-\frac{1}{2}$	115–35
Slow	280–320	1	135–60
Warm	320–40	3	160–70
Moderate	340–70	4	170–85
Fairly hot	370–400	5–6	185–205
Hot	400–40	7	205–25
Very hot	440–80	8–9	225–50

If you are using pictures, try to ensure your words follow their meaning.

In STARTING WITH WATERCOLOURS, Rowland Hilder begins
with some advice on line drawing, giving practical advice
in a clear and interesting way.

EXERCISES IN DRAWING

You learn to draw simply by continuing to draw. While
engaged in drawing practice, you need to be free from worry
and anxiety about the process and free from worry about
the cost of materials, the possible waste of time, whether
or not you are making progress, what people will think of
your work or whether what you are doing is good or bad
and so on.

The cost of materials need not be great. All you need
is plenty of paper and something to draw with. Try a ream
or two of cheap typing paper and an ordinary ballpoint pen.
Begin to draw fearlessly with something that will make a
clear black line.

Draw the things around you: the room, the table laid for
a meal, the view from the window. Just start drawing and
keep on drawing. Draw rapidly and in the first instance do
not be unduly worried about accuracy. If you draw a line
in the wrong place, make a correction on the same drawing
with a bolder, firm line. Aim at making the subject and
the line come alive. At all costs keep going, even if the efforts
do not seem impressive.

Notice the conversational style used: instructions should
give clear information, but also create interest.

Note: solution to I13: repelling sharks

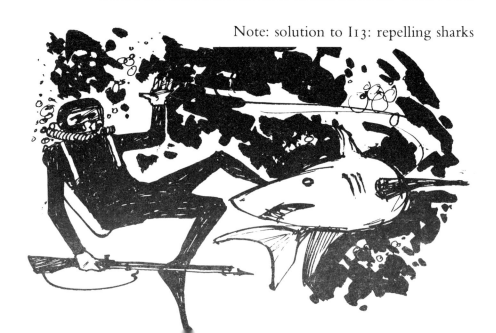

CRITICISM

Some approaches

C1

Look at this picture. It is a painting by Picasso entitled 'Guernica'.

Pablo Picasso, 'Guernica' (1937, May–early June)

Write down your reaction to the painting.

Criticism is concerned with reasoning and making judgements. It is about expressing and understanding opinions, and not taking refuge in easy catch-words and phrases. For example, how often do you hear these words?

'good, fantastic, rubbish, grotty, stupid, crazy, lousy, rotten, amazing, magic, super, nice, all right, not bad, OK, boring.'

Can you add any more to this list?

All these words are used by people when passing an opinion. Broadly, they all mean that something is either good or bad: but beyond that, they hardly mean anything at all. Have you used any of these in your criticism of the painting?

C2

Picasso painted Guernica as a personal response to the bombing of the old market town of Guernica in Spain in April 1937. The town had no military significance during the Spanish Civil War but the German bombers working for Franco used it as a rehearsal for the terror-bombing of civilians which became familiar throughout World War Two.

The painting can therefore be seen as an emotional outburst in protest against the slaughter of defenceless men, women and children. The original is a huge canvas which makes use of a small range of whites and greys.

In the light of this information, you may want to add to or revise your earlier comments.

If you do not like the picture then, of course, say so but avoid using the type of meaningless language referred to in C1.

Try saying an over-worked word ('nice' for example) in as many different ways as possible. Vary the volume, pitch and intonation of your voice.

When a word can mean many different things, or be used in many different ways, it is very difficult to use it so that it means something precise.

Write a dialogue between two people using some of these vague or meaningless words.
They could be:

a) sampling a meal
b) judging a beauty contest
c) looking at a weird painting.

Criticising music can be looked at in two ways:

a) criticism by a 'layman', someone without specialised knowledge
b) criticism by an expert on music, often a musician, who is capable of analysing techniques, method and structure in music. Most of us would come in the first category: we like music which pleases us. Expert knowledge, although interesting, is not vital in being able to form an opinion.

Listen to a current chart 'hit' record. Before writing down your reaction, consider what sort of music you are looking for:
a) music for serious listening
b) music for a discotheque

    c) music for a background to conversation
    d) music for a party.

Discuss the differences between these different types or 'audiences' for music.

What different types of music are needed for a party?

Write down your reaction to the record chosen, bearing in mind what occasion the music is intended for. Also, consider these questions:

    a) Is the singer's voice suited to the type of song?
    b) How does he treat or **use** the lyrics?
    c) Are the lyrics important to the song?
    d) Is the pace, rhythm or power of the music suited to the idea of the song?
    e) Are there any difficult passages in the music that are performed very well or badly (by the lead guitarist, for example)?
    f) What range of instruments is used? Are they used imaginatively and appropriately?

C6

Collect a series of singles/LP tracks together that are suited to the various audiences, and discuss them along the lines indicated in C5.

C7

A record reviewer has a difficult task. In just a few lines he has to give his own reaction to a record, give an impression of what the record contains, and provide some indication of whether it is worth buying.

Here are two examples:

> THE TERMITES: 'I'm gonna crawl'. Drones on, and on. The singer's feline screams don't lift this song out of the doldrums. Crawl back to the studio.

> JUSTIN LEE: 'The Tower'. Trendy, this. Cult-record if ever I saw one. Pretty 12-string work, weird stuff on synthesiser, nice bass and Justin sings OK. Can't understand a word of it.

Discuss the meaning of these reviews. Would these remarks help you in deciding whether to buy the records or not?

C8

Write some short record reviews.
Try writing some in the same 'rock paper' style.

C9

Arrange with a friend that you will both watch the same television programme or film. Try to come to an agreement afterwards on the content of a joint review.

How far have you been able to avoid using some of the 'overworked' words and phrases mentioned earlier? Do they occur more in speech than in writing? We usually use them when giving our **first** reaction to an object – usually an emotional reaction. Having given our first reaction, we then try to think more objectively. We try to put aside our feelings, and really **look** at the object (which may be anything from a car to a poem).

Making a decision

C10

In the following pages, you will find a selection of pictures, articles and news stories concerning Concorde, the world's first supersonic airliner.

We would like you to consider the Concorde project, taking into account the following points:

a) shape, appearance, design
b) comfort, service, convenience
c) noise and environment factors
d) cost of production.

Having looked at the evidence (some of it is conflicting or possibly exaggerated), should Concorde continue to be allowed to fly?

Write an essay in answer to this question.

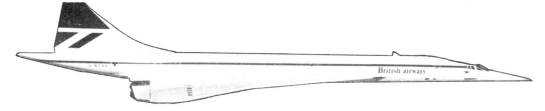

The objections to Concorde are more than merely economic. It is a plane for the wealthy only; it is uneconomic in its use of fossil fuel; it is noisy; and its development has not helped the welfare of mankind as a whole. It is a technological marvel, certainly; and very beautiful. But this does not in itself make it acceptable.

It was, however, solely about the noise of Concorde that I spoke at the Public Hearings in Washington on 5 January 1975, as President of HACAN. I have told the story of that experience elsewhere, together with the transcript of what I said, and this is not the place to repeat them. Two main points stood out from that experience. One was the determination of the British and French media to push Concorde. (I felt this most keenly when THE TIMES came out on its front page with many column inches reporting an attack on me by Lord Boyd Carpenter and Mr Gerald Kaufman, and devoting two lines to my reply.) The other has been the readiness of government to indulge itself in 'terminological inexactitudes' about Concorde. Before those hearings the government had misled the public about the noise of Concorde in replies to parliamentary questions. I fear that the practice has continued. Two examples may be given. Reference was made at the Hearings to the ICAO Assembly Resolution that supersonic aircraft in commercial service will 'not create a noise exceeding the level then accepted for the operation of subsonic aircraft'. Transportation Minister Coleman was told at the Hearings that 'then' referred to 1962, the date when the resolution was passed, whereas the ICAO Bulletin for November 1962 states clearly that 'then' refers to the date when such aircraft would be introduced into commercial service, by which time the noise regulations were far more stringent.

An even more extraordinary example is afforded by the answer given in Parliament to a question on 28 February 1977 concerning the noisiest aircraft to take off from Heathrow in each month since Concorde entered commercial service thirteen months previously. In the answer given, **Concorde was not mentioned**. Mr Richard Wiggs of The Anti-Concorde Project pointed out in a letter in THE TIMES (12 March) that he had got the Civil Aviation Authority to admit that the reason for this was that the Minister's list of the noisiest aircraft had been compiled from the 'noise infringements' at Heathrow – and that since Concorde had been exempted from the Heathrow noise rules it could not infringe them! A further Parliamentary question had been asked, in the hope of putting the record right. In the Minister's second reply (7 March), Concorde appeared as the noisiest aircraft in three months out of thirteen. Mr Wiggs then pointed out that the Concorde noise levels quoted had been measured much further away from the airport than those of the other aircraft, and that the CAA's own published figures showed that when Concorde and the other aircraft were monitored at the same distance (5 km) from start of take-off, Concorde was by far the noisiest aircraft in every month. It was on average more than three times as loud as the loudest subsonic planes (the Boeing 707, and Trident). In the communities at this distance from the airport Concorde's noise was – and is – frequently above the level medically recognized as causing pain in the ears.

It is sad to record such official 'doublethink', and the history of Concorde, when it is later fully told, could well be a matter for national shame as well as national pride. It is unpleasant to record such matters, but a member of a national church must reckon to have duties as well as privileges, and one duty must be not only to praise, but also to expose what dishonours a nation's record.

from TAKING OUR PAST INTO OUR FUTURE
by Hugh Montefiore (Bishop of Birmingham)

Air France Sees Concorde Loss

PARIS, Dec. 12 (AP)—Air France, the French national airline, said today that it expected operation of its Concorde supersonic airliners to show a loss of 86 million francs ($19.3 million) in 1978, up from an earlier forecast of 32 million francs ($7.19 million).

The revised estimate arose from higher maintenance costs and fewer passengers than expected on the Paris-New York run, the company said.

The Concorde was expected to be the only loss on the state-controlled airline's books. Subsonic operations were expected to give Air France a profit of 220 million francs ($49.43 million). Taking into account repayment of investments in the Concorde, the company expects an overall 1978 loss of 331 million francs ($74.38 million) on the supersonic transport.

Air France and British Airways, the British national airline, are the only airlines now flying the Concorde. British Airways has also lost money on the plane. In its annual report dated July 27, the airline said Concorde losses for the fiscal year ended March 31, 1978, were £17 million (then worth $32.3 million).

NEW YORK TIMES, 13 December 1978

CONCORDE DAMAGE: COMMISSION MEETS FRIDAY

Mr Chafic Badre, the Parliamentary Representative for Aley and President of the Parliamentary Commission of Public Works, has summoned the Commission to a meeting next Friday (18/5) to study the question of the damage being caused by the 'bangs' from Concorde in the region of Akkar and Hermel by each overflight of these regions by the Franco-British supersonic.

The Commission should have met yesterday but the meeting was postponed owing to the absence of the Director General of Civil Aviation, Mr Zouheir Beydoun, who is at present out of the country.

Mr Mikhail Daher, the Representative for Akkar, said yesterday that in spite of the promises—all too vague—of those responsible, nothing has been done at the official level to put an end to Concorde overflights across Lebanon which are causing numerous houses to be cracked by the supersonic bangs.

Mr Daher demanded energetic action on the part of the French and British Governments to end the present state of affairs, and to indemnify the owners of damaged property.

Translation, L'ORIENT-LE JOUR, Beirut, 12 May 1979

CONCORDE IN £17 DOGFIGHT

Householder Oswald Page is taking on British Airways in a £17 dog-fight over Concorde.

He claims that vibrations shattered a glass coffee table when the superjet roared low over his home in Old Windsor, Berks.

Mr. Page is trying to collect the compensation from the airline.

He said: 'Concorde was taking off from Heathrow. Vibrations from the engines smashed my table.

'I don't think I'm asking for much, but British Airways have denied responsibility.'

LATEST CONCORDE COSTS

	UK (£ m.)	France (Fr. m.)	Total (£ m.)
DEVELOPMENT			
To end 1975	475	5,841	951
Jan 1, 1976, to completion	89	1,035	203
Total	564	6,876	1,154
PRODUCTION			
To end 1975	199	2,010	—
Jan 1, 1976, to completion	102	1,440	—
Total	301	3,450	—

Development cost is £58 million up on the estimate of 12 months ago. Pay and inflation account for £46 million and changing exchange rates a further £21 million. Engine development is now funded for five years, rather than two, adding £21 million. The British Department of Industry estimates that there has been a small decrease in real costs, about £10 million. Costs up to end-1975 are at prices and exchange rates prevailing when the costs were incurred. Costs to completion of programme are at January 1976 prices; the exchange rate assumed is £1 = Fr9.08.

Taken from a Commons answer last week by Mr Eric Varley, Secretary of State for Industry.

FLIGHT INTERNATIONAL, 10 April 1976

DAILY STAR, Manchester, 20 March 1979

The High Life

The sophisticated cabin service suits the vastly reduced flying times of supersonic travel, and the gourmet meals are served on exclusive tableware. A typical menu might be caviar followed by breast of pheasant Souvarof with endive meunière, fresh asparagus spears and Anna potatoes, followed by Concorde soufflé, cheese board and coffee; accompanied by a choice of apéritifs, wines and liqueurs.

Can you afford *not* to fly Concorde?

Supersonic travel is a reality. Executives with no time to waste are already aware of its overwhelming advantages. Like cutting travelling times by as much as half. Like getting you there ready for work, not ready for bed. (The 'fatigue factors' of long-distance subsonic flying —boredom, stiffness and dehydration— are normally not felt for 10 hours). Like the prestige of being seen to arrive in the world's most advanced form of transportation. All for just more than the normal first class fare across the Atlantic, or 15% more on the Bahrain and Singapore route. Luxurious Concorde may be—an indulgence it is not!

CONCORDE USA: DECISION AWAITED

US Secretary of Transportation William T. Coleman's public hearing in Washington to consider the request for Concorde landing rights in Washington and New York occupied ten hours and just over seventy witnesses: about thirty for Concorde and forty against. Most observers agreed that no witness on either side had presented any argument or fact that had not been heard many times before . . .

During the hearing Coleman pointed out that Concorde complied with all of the regulations in force at the time it was designed and that it would be unreasonable to expect any manufacturer to do more. He also alluded to US obligations to allow landing rights as long as the aircraft complied with existing regulations, and to the fact that there are no noise standards for SSTs. He also mentioned that the US was developing such standards, and said that the Environmental Protection Agency had recommended to him that the first sixteen Concordes should be exempted from those noise standards.

Conceding that 'noise is the main issue,' Kaufman reiterated that evidence is on record showing Concorde noise characteristics to be comparable to those of the narrow-bodied long-range jets.

British Aircraft Corporation Concorde project director Mr Michael Wilde amplified Mr Kaufman's remarks, explained the 'noise-exposure forecast' concept (which produces contours of equal cumulative noise-exposure around the airport), and showed charts (taken directly from the EIS) of NEF 30 and NEF 40 contours at New York Kennedy and Washington Dulles airports, with and without Concorde operations. With four daily Concorde services into New York (eight additional movements in an average total of over 1,000 per day) ' the area change is negligible and we are told that the affected population increases by 2,000—about four-tenths of one per cent.' Similar charts for Washington Dulles show less than 1,000 people affected within the NEF 30 contour and the inclusion of Concorde operations produces little increase in area and none in affected population.

Discussing single-event footprints, he said that these contours 'do not and cannot present a proper perspective of the noise effect of the proposed services. People react to the frequency of hearing a noise and the time of day at which they hear it, much more than to the loudness of one single noise.

'The simplifying assumptions (suggested by BAC to the FAA) in the Concorde data lead to much greater misrepresentations of the single-event footprint areas—they lead to an exaggeration by more than forty per cent at the 100EPNdB level in some cases and by even greater percentages at the 110EPNdB level.'

M Roger Chevalier, a senior vice-president of Aérospatiale, emphasised that pollution problems were by no means unique to supersonic aircraft. He observed that the ozone layer in the northern hemisphere increased in thickness during the decade up to 1970 and cast doubt on the theories which suggest that a decrease should have occurred. 'In truth, the current models have not been confirmed experimentally, and it is almost certain that the most pessimistic models are wrong.'

Although the US Environmental Protection Agency has officially recommended that Mr Coleman deny Concorde landing rights at both Kennedy and Dulles airports, it might be satisfied with the decision which most observers expect. That would allow operations to Washington to begin in 1976, while forbidding or postponing operations at Kennedy.

Art

C11

Look at the picture below, 'Death's Door.' It is an etching by Louis Schiavonetti from an original by William Blake.

What guidelines would you use for criticising this picture? How far would they differ from those used in criticising a practical object, such as Concorde? Do you need to have the picture explained to you before you can comment upon it?

C12

We would like you to consider two further paintings: Kishi Ganku's 'Tiger by a Stream' (front cover) and 'When Did You Last See Your Father?' by W. F. Yeames (below).

The paintings differ in terms of the feelings the artists wish to arouse in us.

C13

Write down your first reaction to Kishi Ganku's painting. Then discuss it. You may like to consider the following: the artist's use of strong colour, and the way in which he has portrayed the tiger's ferocity and lithe movement.

Write about the picture, describing the scene it portrays, and your feelings about it.

C14

'When Did You Last See Your Father?' is also intended to be a pleasing picture to look at; but, something significant is clearly happening in the picture as well. Are we meant to sympathise with the boy in the centre?

In a small group of students, reproduce the scene.

How has the artist arranged the people and furniture in order to put emphasis on the boy?

Using the title of the picture as an opening line, improvise or script the scene.

Prose

The writer's task is similar to that of the painter. 'Word-artist' would be a fair description of his or her function, although a writer can bring movement and speech to the scenes he or she creates.

In NETWORK ONE we also considered the question of critical choice. We can prefer one painting or piece of writing to another, just as we may prefer the style and colour of one pair of shoes to another.

Below there are two descriptions of a winter landscape:

WINTER FANTASY

Winter silences are deep. The
earth with frost is bound. Ice
becalms the singing brooks, and on
the frozen ground – snowflakes fall
like fairy foam that piles up
feather-light – till every bush is
hidden under mounds of dazzling
white.

Winter is the silent season,
quietening the mind. You who walk
the country lanes a new delight
will find – as you tramp
soft-footed into scenes of fantasy
– the well-known way dissolves
into a world of mystery. The
blinding snow obliterates the
once-familiar view – and you are
lost, a stranger in a place you
thought you knew.

Patience Strong (WOMAN's OWN, 12 February 1979)

... snow was general all over Ireland. It was falling on every part of the bog of Allen and, further westwards, softly falling into the dark mutinous Shannon waves. It was falling, too,

upon every part of the lonely churchyard on the hill where
Michael Furey lay buried. It lay thickly drifted on the
crooked crosses and headstones, on the spears of the little
gate, on the barren thorns.

from THE DEAD by James Joyce

Compare these two passages.
Which of them succeeds in creating the clearer picture of
a winter landscape? Which of them employs the more
effective descriptive language?
Are these writers intending their pieces for the same type
of audience?
Discuss the methods used by each writer.
Is rhythm important in either of the two pieces?

C17

Write your own prose description of a winter landscape –
this photograph may be a suitable subject. Experiment with
some of the methods used by the writers above.

C18

Images are used by writers to give the reader a clear idea of the object or feeling the writer is describing.

Similes and metaphors are often used by writers. We use them too in conversation. Can you think of some examples? (Refer to the section on 'Description'.) As critics, we have to decide whether images 'work', and if not, why not. For example, consider these short descriptions of guests at a New Year's Eve party:

> Then I went back to the noisy circle of clasped hands; to Don and Eve, from next door, misty-eyed with the joy of having patched up their latest quarrel; Julia and Michael, both bare-footed, with freaked-out hairdoes; Aunt Grace, like an animated ramrod; my charming bachelor cousin Oliver; and all the odds and ends of people we always scooped up for New Year because they liked to share it with us.

> Audrie Manley-Tucker
> WOMAN AND HOME, February 1979

How clear an idea do you have of the appearance and character of these guests? Discuss the possible meaning of the simile 'like an animated ramrod' as applied to Aunt Grace.

C19

Write a similar short piece concerning people at a party you have been to. Try using some short similes that give a clear idea or picture of the people you describe.

C20

Set up such a party scene in drama. Work out some dialogue along the lines of the characters you have in mind. Use the idea of jealousy for a story or plot line. One of your characters may be described as 'catty' or a 'stirrer'. What kind of person do these words suggest? What movements would they have? What mode of speech? How would they be dressed?

C21

By now, you may have encountered some questions which are difficult to answer.

a) What is the difference between 'good' and 'bad' writing?
b) If a book, painting or record has become famous, does that mean that it **must** be of high quality?
c) In any of the passages you have read so far, have you felt that the writer was being 'insincere'?
d) Does a writer write purely to earn money?

Look at some of your own written work.

a) Do you write for yourself?
b) Do you write to please the teacher?
c) Do you write to entertain the teacher?
d) Do you write to earn good marks?
e) Why does your work succeed sometimes and fail sometimes?
f) Your English teacher is a critic. What does he or she look for in your writing?

Some guidelines: when reading prose, poetry or drama:

Look for images, similes and metaphors which are 'fresh' – not over-worked and familiar clichés – original, and appropriate.

Look for dialogue which is realistic, interesting and appropriate to the character using it.

Look for descriptions of characters which provide both clear visual images and **insight** into the people portrayed; characters which are three-dimensional and not simply 'flat'.

Look for description of rooms, houses, landscape, which uses important and striking detail, and does not simply conjure up a Christmas-card type cliché picture.

Ernest Hemingway's short story THE END OF SOMETHING describes how Nick Adams ends his relationship with his girl Marjorie:

THE END OF SOMETHING

In the old days Hortons Bay was a lumbering town. No one who lived in it was out of sound of the big saws in the mill by the lake. Then one year there were no more logs to make lumber. The lumber schooners came into the bay and were loaded with the cut of the mill that stood stacked in the yard. All the piles of lumber were carried away. The big mill building had all its machinery that was removable taken out and hoisted on board one of the schooners by the men who had worked in the mill. The schooner moved out of the bay toward the open lake carrying the two great saws, the travelling carriage that hurled the logs against the revolving, circular saws, and all the rollers, wheels, belts and iron piled on a hull-deep load of lumber. Its open hold covered with canvas and lashed tight, the sails of the schooner filled and it moved out into the open lake, carrying with it everything that had made the mill a mill and Hortons Bay a town.

The one-story bunk houses, the eating-house, the company store, the mill offices and the big mill itself stood deserted in the acres of sawdust that covered the swampy meadow by the shore of the bay.

Ten years later there was nothing of the mill left except the broken white limestone of its foundations showing through the swampy second growth as Nick and Marjorie rowed along the shore. They were trolling along the edge of the channel bank where the bottom dropped off suddenly from sandy shallows to twelve feet of dark water. They were trolling on their way to the point to set night lines for rainbow trout.

'There's our old ruin, Nick', Marjorie said.

Nick, rowing, looked at the white stone in the green trees.

'There it is', he said.

'Can you remember when it was a mill?' Marjorie asked.

'I can just remember', Nick said.

'It seems more like a castle', Marjorie said.

Nick said nothing. They rowed on out of sight of the mill, following the shore line. Then Nick cut across the bay.

'They aren't striking', he said.

'No', Marjorie said. She was intent on the rod all the time they trolled, even when she talked. She loved to fish. She loved to fish with Nick.

Close beside the boat a big trout broke the surface of the water. Nick pulled hard on one oar so the boat would turn and the bait spinning far behind would pass where the trout was feeding. As the trout's back came up out of the water the minnows jumped wildly. They sprinkled the surface like a handful of shot thrown into the water. Another trout broke water, feeding on the other side of the boat.

'They're feeding', Marjorie said.

'But they won't strike'. Nick said.

He rowed the boat around to troll past both the feeding fish, then headed it for the point. Marjorie did not reel in until the boat touched the shore.

They pulled the boat up the beach and Nick lifted out a pail of live perch. The perch swam in the water in the pail. Nick caught three of them with his hands and cut their heads off and skinned them while Marjorie chased with her hands in the bucket, finally caught a perch, cut its head off and skinned it. Nick looked at her fish.

'You don't want to take the ventral fin out', he said. 'It'll be all right for bait but it's better with the ventral fin in.'

He hooked each of the skinned perch through the tail. There were two hooks attached to a leader on each rod. Then Marjorie rowed the boat out over the channel-bank, holding the line in her teeth, and looking toward Nick, who

stood on the shore holding the rod and letting the line run
out from the reel.

'That's about right', he called.

'Should I let it drop?' Marjorie called back, holding the
line in her hand.

'Sure. Let it go.' Marjorie dropped the line overboard and
watched the baits go down through the water.

She came in with the boat and ran the second line out
the same way. Each time Nick set a heavy slab of driftwood
across the butt of the rod to hold it solid and propped it
up at an angle with a small slab. He reeled in the slack line
so the line ran taut out to where the bait rested on the sandy
floor of the channel and set the click on the reel. When a
trout, feeding on the bottom, took the bait it would run
with it, taking line out of the reel in a rush and making
the reel sing with the click on.

Marjorie rowed up the point a little way so she would
not disturb the line. She pulled hard on the oars and the
boat went way up the beach. Little waves came in with it.
Marjorie stepped out of the boat and Nick pulled the boat
high up the beach.

'What's the matter, Nick?' Marjorie asked.

'I don't know', Nick said, getting wood for a fire.

They made a fire with driftwood. Marjorie went to the
boat and brought a blanket. The evening breeze blew the
smoke toward the point, so Marjorie spread the blanket out
between the fire and the lake.

Marjorie sat on the blanket with her back to the fire and
waited for Nick. He came over and sat down beside her
on the blanket. In back of them was the close second-growth
timber of the point and in front was the bay with the mouth
of Hortons Creek. It was not quite dark. The fire-light went
as far as the water. They could both see the two steel rods
at an angle over the dark water. The fire glinted on the
reels.

Marjorie unpacked the basket of supper.

'I don't feel like eating', said Nick.

'Come on and eat, Nick.'

'All right.'

They ate without talking, and watched the two rods and
the fire-light in the water.

'There's going to be a moon to-night', said Nick. He
looked across the bay to the hills that were beginning to
sharpen against the sky. Beyond the hills he knew the moon
was coming up.

'I know it', Marjorie said happily.

'You know everything', Nick said.

'Oh, Nick, please cut it out! Please, please don't be that way!'

'I can't help it', Nick said. 'You do. You know everything. That's the trouble. You know you do.'

Marjorie did not say anything.

'I've taught you everything. You know you do. What don't you know, anyway?'

'Oh, shut up', Marjorie said. 'There comes the moon.'

They sat on the blanket without touching each other and watched the moon rise.

'You don't have to talk silly', Marjorie said. 'What's really the matter?'

'I don't know.'

'Of course you know.'

'No, I don't.'

'Go on and say it.'

Nick looked on at the moon, coming up over the hills.

'It isn't fun any more.'

He was afraid to look at Marjorie. Then he looked at her. She sat there with her back toward him. He looked at her back. 'It isn't fun any more. Not any of it.'

She didn't say anything. He went on. 'I feel as though everything was gone to hell inside of me. I don't know, Marge. I don't know what to say.'

He looked on at her back.

'Isn't love any fun?' Marjorie said.

'No', Nick said. Marjorie stood up. Nick sat there, his head in his hands.

'I'm going to take the boat', Marjorie called to him. 'You can walk back around the point.'

'All right', Nick said. 'I'll push the boat off for you.'

'You don't need to', she said. She was afloat in the boat on the water with the moonlight on it. Nick went back and lay down with his face in the blanket by the fire. He could hear Marjorie rowing on the water.

He lay there for a long time. He lay there while he heard Bill come into the clearing walking around through the woods. He felt Bill coming up to the fire. Bill didn't touch him, either.

'Did she go all right', Bill said.

'Yes', Nick said, lying his face on the blanket.

'Have a scene?'

'No, there wasn't any scene.'

'How do you feel?'

'Oh, go away, Bill! Go away for a while.'

Bill selected a sandwich from the lunch basket and walked over to have a look at the rods.

Ernest Hemingway

C24

Discuss Hemingway's story, bearing in mind the guidelines mentioned in C23. It is important, however, at this point to understand the different ways in which the novelist and short story writer must work.

> It follows that, unlike the novelist, who can lead the reader through two or three hundred pages, the short story writer must make his effects quickly because space is limited. He doesn't, as the novelist does, deal with the development of characters ... he catches them at a time of crisis or decision, at some turning point in their lives, and he must engage the reader's attention immediately with his opening. And ... he must nevertheless leave the reader with a sense of completeness at the end.

from ON WRITING THESE STORIES by Stan Barstow
(Longman Imprint edition)

Has Hemingway 'engaged the reader's attention immediately'? How has he attempted to do this? What is the purpose of the description of the mill?

Is the vocabulary varied, simple, or complex?

C25

With a friend, write or improvise a script using the dialogue that Hemingway has written.

Discuss other ways in which Nick could have ended the relationship.

C26

Write a short criticism of Hemingway's story.

C27

Short stories published in magazines are written for a specific purpose and for a specific market. These factors should be remembered when criticising the following piece:

Name: Sandra Lawton
Age: 18 **Birthplace:** Worcester

When Sandra became a member of The Family, she thought she'd found true happiness...

COMMUNE OF CRIME!

IT had been a terrible row. The worst I'd ever had with Mum.

'I just don't know what to say to you, Sandra,' she'd moaned. 'You need a father to keep you under control!'

I'd stormed out, and taken the next bus into town. Then I wandered around with my hastily packed suitcase, wondering where on earth I was going to stay.

Was this what I'd really wanted? It was certainly what the row had been about. I'd told Mum I wanted to get away from our tiny village. That I thought there had to be something more to life than being buried there.

After all, Dad had lived all his life there, died there—what was the point?

Tears came to my eyes as I remembered him. I wandered aimlessly along the crowded street until suddenly out of the blue, I heard a voice . . .

'Are you lost, love? That's the trouble today, isn't it? Everybody's lost. Nobody can find their way.'

SCRUFFY

I stopped and looked up. In front of me was this guy with long black hair and scruffy clothes. He looked quite a bit older than me.

His face was lined and suntanned, as though he'd lived a lot and knew a lot.

And his eyes were bright— almost black in colour. They stared at me and seemed to see straight through me.

He handed me a pamphlet. I saw it was about something called the 'Family of Truth'. But I threw it away and dodged into a coffee bar.

But he just followed me in and sat down, too. When he asked me what was wrong, I couldn't help myself. I just poured everything out—about Mum, my boring meaningless life, poor Dad—the lot.

And then he started to talk. He had a lovely, soft voice. It was almost hypnotic. It made me want to curl up and go to sleep. It made me feel safe and warm, the way I had when Dad had told me bed-time stories.

He told me he lived in a commune on a farm. He said he was the father of a big family, people like me who wanted to find some meaning in life.

They had no possessions, they shared everything. They lived by growing crops, organically he said, which meant they didn't polute the soil with chemicals. They lived in perfect peace.

It sounded like the promised land, so different from home . . .

His name was Damian and he called me his lost little girl.

He was the most wonderful person I'd ever met. He wouldn't let me down like other boys I'd known.

I left with him, and in his battered truck we drove to the isolated farm where his family lived.

It wasn't as homely as I'd imagined. All the people—about twenty of them, looked scruffy and I had to share a room with two other girls.

KISS

But before I went to bed, Damian came and kissed me. I could tell that I was something special to him, but the other girls didn't seem to mind, even though they all obviously worshipped him.

All except one. Marian. She hardly said a word to anyone. She looked miserable, but everyone else looked really happy.

The next morning I got a shock. I was woken at five, and I had to learn to milk a cow. And after that, I discovered what organic farming meant. We couldn't use chemical fertilizers, so we had to spread cow dung on the land.

...THE OH BOY CASEBOOK...

At the end of the day I was whacked. Damian didn't work like the others.

'I have to meditate,' he explained. 'I sit and concentrate on all our problems, and in the end I know how to solve them.'

In the evening, we sat around. There was no electricity, only candles, and there was a smell of incense in the air.

Damian played his guitar and sang songs to us. And then he talked. I lost the meaning of his words after a few minutes. He was talking about our souls and our family, and peace and love.

But his voice was like music. It seemed to vibrate through my whole body and I drifted into a dream world. I knew I loved him.

Life went on like this for about a month. The only time I left the farm was when Damian drove me into town, so I could draw my savings out of the Post Office. I gave all the money to him. We had no possessions. We shared everything . . .

Then one day, I was just coming in from the fields when I saw Damian driving up to the farmhouse. He'd been into town to sell our produce. And to my suprise, he had a girl with him.

'Meet our new sister,' he said, and then they went into his room. I saw him touch her cheek. I knew he was sitting in there playing his guitar and singing to her—the way he'd done with me nearly every night up till now.

And I'd thought he loved *me* in a special kind of way. But now he'd replaced me.

I sat for an hour in my room. I could hear the soft melodic sound of his voice. Tears came to my eyes. It was like my Dad dying all over again. I felt all alone in the world.

I couldn't stand it any more. I got up and burst in on them. And found them locked in a passionate kiss!

'Damian . . . what's happening?' I cried. 'You never kiss anyone but me. How can you kiss her?'

'Get out!' he yelled, his dark eyes blazing. 'We share everything. That means you have to share me. I kiss who I like!'

'He wouldn't let me down like other boys . . .'

SHOCK

Next day I felt terrible. I felt I'd betrayed him. I'd been greedy, wanting to have him all to myself. That wasn't the idea of the place at all.

I knocked on his door and went in.

He was lying in bed, drinking whisky. There was a half-empty bottle beside the bed.

I was shocked. 'Why are you drinking?' I asked. 'You said it was wrong. Why aren't you meditating? Or working like the rest of us?'

'It's hard on the brain, love, is meditation,' he said, almost mocking me. 'Now leave me to relax!'

I backed out, puzzled, and in tears. Then I saw Marian, the miserable girl who never spoke.

She sneered at me. 'Oh, so you've finally twigged about Damian, have you?' she said. 'He always takes up with any new girl till he's got her under his thumb.

'He's got all our money, too. So that when he's got enough he'll sell this place. He only grows organic food 'cos he can sell it at high prices in health food shops.

'And he doesn't meditate either. He drinks, and picks out bets on horse races. He's a lazy good-for-nothing crook, that's all! He's fooled you like he's fooled the rest of us!'

'But if you hate him, why stay?' I asked, not wanting to believe her.

SPELL

'My folks won't have me back. They came here to get me once, and I wouldn't go. I was still under his spell. But you can get out, while you've got a home to go to!'

She was crying so bitterly, I didn't need telling again. She had some money hidden away, and gave me enough to get home . . .

Mum was so pleased to see me, and I'm happier at home now. Oh, it's still not perfect. But I've learned that *nowhere* is. You have to work at things to be happy.

And sometimes looking for something perfect can make you more miserable.

I've cried a lot over being betrayed by Damian. But it could have been worse. I might have been trapped there, like poor Marian . . .

Reproduced by permission of IPC Magazines Ltd., publishers of 'Oh Boy'

Write down your initial reaction to the story. Is there anything in the way that it is written and presented that implies it is autobiographical?

Have you assumed the story is 'true'? If so, in what ways has this affected your response to it? Did you become involved in the writing? Did you identify with Sandra?

C28 Discuss the piece, focussing on the dialogue and quality of description; discuss whether you find the characters 'realistic' or 'stereotyped'.

C29 THE END OF SOMETHING and COMMUNE OF CRIME are both concerned with the ending of an affair, but the stories are written in different ways. List these differences.

C30 Improvise the scene in which Sandra sees Damian with the other girl, and finally meets Marian. Use dialogue from the story and discuss its effectiveness.

C31 A writer can also employ a very effective and dramatic technique of writing something as if it were recorded in the mind of (or spoken by) the main character in the story. This method is known as 'stream of consciousness' writing (see 'Narrative' section N5).

Stan Barstow uses this technique in his humorous story THE HUMAN ELEMENT. Here Harry West, who works as a fitter, has unwillingly agreed to accompany his landlady Mrs Baynes, her husband and daughter Thelma on a picnic.

> In about twenty minutes we're well out in the country and we get off the bus and cross the road and take a path through a field of corn that's ready for getting in, it's so heavy and ripe, and as still as if we were seeing it on a photo. It's a real scorcher of a day. We go round the edge of the farmyard and down into the woods. The trees come over and shut the sun out and the path's narrow and steep. We walk in single file with Ma Baynes in front and every now and then one of us trips over the roots that stick out of the ground all hard and shiny like the veins on the backs of old people's hands. After a bit of this we come out into

a clearing. Down the hill we can see the beck with the sun
shining on it and on the far side there's a golf course with
one or two nobs having a game. Past that there's fields
stretching miles off and electricity pylons marching along
like something out of a science-fiction picture.

'This'll do', Ma Baynes says and drops her bag and flops
down on the grass like half a ton of sand. Old Man Baynes
shoots me a look and I pass the radio over. He takes it out
of the case and switches on, stretching out on the grass with
his ear stuck right up to the speaker as though he thinks
the set's too little to make much noise.

Ma Baynes levers her shoes off and pushes the hair off
her forehead. Then she clasps her hands in her lap and gives
a satisfied look all round.

'We sh'd come here more often', she says, ' 'stead o'
stickin' in that mucky old town.' She gives Thelma and me
a funny look. 'Me an' your father used to come courtin'
here', she says. 'Didn't we, George?'

Old Man Baynes just says, 'Mmmm?' and Ma Baynes
twists her head and pins him with a real sharp look.

'I hope you're not goin' to have your head stuck inside
that thing all afternoon', she says. 'If that's all you can find
to do you might as well ha' stopped at home.'

'That's what I wanted to do', he says, and gives the radio
a tap with his finger. 'I can't get no reception.' He picks
the set up and gives it a shake.

'Here', I say, 'let me.'

Ma Baynes gives a sigh. 'Here we are, next to nature,
an' all they can find to do is fiddle wi' a wireless set!'

After a bit she sends Thelma up to the farm for a jug
of tea. By this time me and Old Man Baynes between us
have taken so many parts out of the radio it'd take a chopper
to strip it down any more. All the guts of it are spread out
in one of my hankies on the grass and I'm looking at them
in a bit of a daze, wondering if we haven't gone a bit too
far.

Old Man Baynes has lost all interest. He's sitting by himself, looking out over the valley, chewing grass stalks and
muttering to himself something like, 'I wonder how they're
gettin' on . . .' He's worried sick about that cricket match.

Soon Thelma comes back with the tea and Ma Baynes
sets the mugs out. 'Come on, you men, and get your teas.'

We get going on the fishpaste sandwiches. Nobody has
much to say now. It's all right going out into the country,
but what do you do when you get there? It begins to get

me down after a bit and I get to thinking about the bike and all I could be doing with her if I wasn't wasting my time sitting here.

When we've finished Thelma picks up the jug.

'I'll take that back, if you like', I say. I think a walk might help to pass the time.

Ma Baynes looks up at us. 'Why don't you both go?'

I'd rather go on my own, but I give a shrug. 'If you like.'

We set off up the path under the trees. It's a bit cooler here but I'm still sweating a lot and my shirt's stuck to me. Thelma's the same. Her frock was tight to start with and now it looks as if it's been pasted on her. We get the full force of the sun as we leave the shade on the edge of the farmyard, and it's dazzling the way it bounces back off the whitewashed walls. Everything's dead quiet and there's no sign of life except for a few hens pecking around and a great red rooster strutting about among them as though he owns the place. I put my hand down on the flagstones as Thelma comes back from the house.

'Could fry your breakfast on here', I say, just to help the conversation on a bit.

'It is hot, in't it?' she says, and flaps her arms about like an angry old hen. 'I wish we was at the seaside; I'd love to be in the sea just now.'

Stan Barstow

The passage is written in the same descriptive style that Harry would use when re-telling the incident.

  a) Write down some of the similes used in the passage. Are they the type that Harry would use when describing the incident to someone else?
  b) Why has the passage been written in the present tense?
  c) What impression is given from the passage of the character of Ma Baynes? What methods has Barstow used to suggest her character?
  d) Note down any phrases which introduce humour into the passage.

C32

In the following passage from DOMBEY & SON, Charles Dickens suffuses the mood of despair felt by Mr Dombey with the experience of his journey by steam train.

The very speed at which the train was whirled along mocked the swift course of the young life that had been borne away so steadily and so inexorably to its fore-doomed end. The power that forced itself upon its iron way – its own – defiant of all paths and roads, piercing through the heart of every obstacle, and dragging living creatures of all classes, ages, and degrees behind it, was a type of the triumphant monster, Death.

Away, with a shriek, and a roar, and a rattle, from the town, burrowing among the dwellings of men and making the streets hum, flashing out into the meadows for a moment, mining in through the damp earth, booming on in darkness and heavy air, bursting out again into the sunny day so bright and wide; away, with a shriek, and a roar, and a rattle, through the fields, through the woods, through the corn, through the hay, through the chalk, through the mould, through the clay, through the rock, among objects close at hand and almost in the grasp, ever flying from the traveller, and a deceitful distance ever moving slowly within him: like as in the track of the remorseless monster, Death!

Through the hollow, on the height, by the heath, by the orchard, by the park, by the garden, over the canal, across the river, where the sheep are feeding, where the mill is going, where the barge is floating, where the dead are lying, where the factory is smoking, where the stream is running, where the village clusters, where the great cathedral rises, where the bleak moor lies, and the wild breeze smooths or ruffles it at its inconstant will; away, with a shriek, and a roar, and a rattle, and no trace to leave behind but dust and vapour: like as in the track of the remorseless monster, Death!

Breasting the wind and light, the shower and sunshine, away, and still away, it rolls and roars, fierce and rapid, smooth and certain, and great works and massive bridges crossing up above, fall like a beam of shadow an inch broad, upon the eye, and then are lost. Away, and still away, onward and onward ever: glimpses of cottage-homes, of houses, mansions, rich estates, of husbandry and handicraft, of people, of old roads and paths that look deserted, small, and insignificant as they are left behind: and so they do, and what else is there but such glimpses, in the track of the indomitable monster, Death!

Away, with a shriek, and a roar, and a rattle, plunging down into the earth again, and working on in such a storm of energy and perseverance, that amidst the darkness and whirlwind the motions seems reversed, and to tend furiously backward, until a ray of light upon the wet wall shows its surface flying past like a fierce stream. Away once more into the day, and through the day, with a shrill yell of exultation, roaring, rattling, tearing on, spurning everything with its dark breath, sometimes pausing for a minute where a crowd of faces are, that in a minute more are not: sometimes lapping water greedily, and before the spout at which it drinks has ceased to drip upon the ground, shrieking, roaring, rattling through the purple distance!

Louder and louder yet, it shrieks and cries as it comes tearing on resistless to the goal: and now its way, still like the way of Death, is strewn with ashes thickly. Everything around is blackened. There are dark pools of water, muddy lanes, and miserable habitations far below. There are jagged walls and falling houses close at hand, and through the battered roofs and broken windows, wretched rooms are seen, where want and fever hide themselves in many wretched shapes, while smoke and crowded gables, and distorted chimneys, and deformity of brick and mortar penning up deformity of mind and body, choke the murky distance. As Mr Dombey looks out of his carriage window, it is never in his thoughts that the monster who has brought him there has let the light of day in on these things: not made or caused them. It was the journey's fitting end, and might have been the end of everything; it was so ruinous and dreary.

Charles Dickens

Write a criticism of the passage, paying attention to Dickens' use of rhythm, repetition, sentence length, punctuation and vocabulary suggesting the movement of the train.

Note down any similarities or differences between the methods employed by Dickens and Barstow.

C33

Read the following extract from Jonathan Swift's essay A MODEST PROPOSAL.

The number of Souls in this Kingdom being usually reckoned one Million and a half, Of these I calculate there may be about two hundred thousand Couple whose Wives are Breeders; from which number I substract thirty Thousand Couples, who are able to maintain their own Children, although I apprehend there cannot be so many, under the present Distresses of the Kingdom; but this being granted, there will remain an hundred and seventy thousand Breeders. I again Substract fifty Thousand, for those Women who miscarry, or whose Children die by accident, or disease within the Year. There only remain an hundred and twenty thousand Children of poor Parents annually born: The question therefore is, How this number shall be reared, and provided for? which, as I have already said, under the present Situation of Affairs, is utterly impossible by all the Methods hitherto proposed; for we can neither employ them in Handicraft or Agriculture; we neither build Houses, (I mean in the Country) nor cultivate Land: They can very seldom pick up a Livelihood by Stealing till they arrive at six years Old; except where they are of towardly parts; although, I confess, they learn the Rudiments much earlier; during which time they can however be properly looked upon only as Probationers; as I have been informed by a principal Gentleman in the County of Cavan, who protested to me, that he never knew above one or two Instances under the Age of six, even in a part of the Kingdom so renowned for the quickest proficiency in that Art.

I am assured by our Merchants, that a Boy or a Girl before twelve years Old, is no saleable Commodity, and even when they come to this Age, they will not yield above three Pounds, or three Pounds and half a Crown at most, on the Exchange; which cannot turn to Account either to the Parents or Kingdom, the Charge of Nutriment and Rags having been at least four times that Value.

I shall now therefore humbly propose my own Thoughts, which I hope will not be liable to the least Objection.

I have been assured by a very knowing American of my acquaintance in London, that a young healthy Child well Nursed is at a year Old a most delicious nourishing and wholesome Food, whether Stewed, Roasted, Baked, or Boiled; and I make no doubt that it will equally serve in a Fricasie, or a Ragoust.

I do therefore humbly offer it to publick consideration, that of the Hundred and twenty thousand Children, already computed, twenty thousand may be reserved for Breed, whereof only one fourth part to be Males; which is more than we allow to Sheep, black Cattle, or Swine, and my Reason is, that these Children are seldom the Fruits of Marriage, a Circumstance not much regarded by our Savages, therefore, one Male will be sufficient to serve four Females. That the remaining Hundred thousand may at a

year Old be offered in Sale to the Persons of Quality and
Fortune, through the Kingdom, always advising the Mother
to let them Suck plentifully in the last Month, so as to render
them Plump, and Fat for a good Table. A Child will make
two Dishes at an Entertainment for Friends, and when the
Family dines alone, the fore or hind Quarter will make a
reasonable Dish, and seasoned with a little Pepper or Salt
will be very good Boiled on the fourth Day, especially in
Winter.

I have reckoned upon a Medium, that a Child just born
will weigh 12 pounds, and in a solar Year, if tolerably nursed,
encreaseth to 28 Pounds.

I grant this food will be somewhat dear, and therefore
very proper for Landlords, who, as they have already de-
voured most of the Parents seem to have the best Title to

the Children.

Infant's flesh will be in Season throughout the Year, but more plentiful in March, and a little before and after; for we are told by a grave Author an eminent French Physician, that Fish being a prolifick Dyet, there are more Children born in Roman Catholick Countries about nine Months after Lent, than at any other Season; therefore reckoning a Year after Lent, the Markets will be more glutted than usual, because the Number of Popish Infants, is at least three to one in this Kingdom, and therefore it will have one other Collateral advantage, by lessening the Number of Papists among us.

I have already computed the Charge of nursing a Begger's Child (in which List I reckon all Cottagers, Labourers, and four fifths of the Farmers) to be about two Shillings per Annum, Rags included; and I believe no Gentleman would repine to give Ten Shillings for the Carcass of a good fat Child, which, as I have said will make four Dishes of excellent Nutritive Meat, when he hath only some particular Friend, or his own Family to dine with him. Thus the Squire will learn to be a good Landlord, and grow popular among his Tenants, the Mother will have Eight Shillings neat Profit, and be fit for Work till she produces another Child.

Those who are more thrifty (as I must confess the Times require) may flay the Carcass; the Skin of which, Artificially dressed, will make admirable Gloves for Ladies, and Summer Boots for fine Gentlemen.

As to our City of Dublin, Shambles may be appointed for this purpose, in the most convenient parts of it, and Butchers we may be assured will not be wanting; although I rather recommend buying the Children alive, and dressing them hot from the Knife, as we do roasting Pigs.

A very worthy Person, a true Lover of his Country, and whose Virtues I highly esteem, was lately pleased, in discoursing on this matter, to offer a refinement upon my Scheme. He said, that many Gentlemen of this Kingdom, having of late destroyed their Deer, he conceived that the Want of Venison might be well supply'd by the Bodies of young Lads and Maidens, not exceeding fourteen Years of Age, nor under twelve; so great a Number of both Sexes in every Country being now ready to Starve, for want of Work and Service: And these to be disposed of by their Parents if alive, or otherwise by their nearest Relations.

Jonathan Swift

Check the meaning of the word 'satire', which has been used to describe the passage.

a) Note down any words or phrases which suggest that Swift is being satirical.

b) Discuss the meaning of the passage. What is Swift's purpose? What feelings is he trying to arouse in the reader?

c) Which of the following words adequately describes the style and tone of the passage: poetic, lyrical, conventional, pompous, ironic?

d) Why has Swift used such a style when writing about such a gruesome subject?

e) At which sections of society is Swift aiming his satire? What impression of society is he trying to convey?

f) Write a letter (possibly in the same style) rebuking Swift for his 'poor taste' in writing the essay, and defending those whom he has attacked.

C34

Many contemporary books carry with them short comments such as:

'Do not read this, if you have bad dreams!'

'These are stories to be read with the light on!'

'A story of tender passionate romance touched with the tragedy of grief.'

'Good living, sex and violent action . . . a thundering good story.'

Such comments are used as inducements for people to buy books, but they often appear initially in book reviews published by the press.

A review usually contains a summary of the contents or story-line, general comments on the quality of the book, the writer's style and method.

You should remember when writing a book review, that you are writing for the benefit of others who wish to know whether the book in question would make good reading for them. There should be a balance of information and reasonably objective comments.

Collect a series of book reviews that you have written together in a file and place them in the class library so that library users can refer to them when selecting books.

Poetry

Perhaps it is impossible to define poetry or even to say how it differs from prose. However, it does have some features which you may like to consider as you work through the following assignments:

a) Poetry is often economical in the use of words.
b) There is a high degree of selectivity about the words a poet uses.
c) Patterning words on the paper counts for much whilst the conventional rules of grammar and punctuation may not always be regarded.
d) A poem is often suggestive and open to a wide variety of interpretations.

Read the poem below, and write down your first reaction to it.

SLEEPWALKER

He found her
Standing,
Balanced between two steps
Her thin face
Angular and glowing white
In the overflow
Of light from his bedroom,
Eyes shut,
Unconscious of her movements.
He took
Her arm
– Her skin was cool to the touch,
And guided her upwards
Safe to the haven of her bed
Wondering what dream
Had brought her into the cold hall
And wishing it was as easy
To guide her during her waking hours
As when she slept.

Rachel Smithers (aged sixteen)

Read your notes to the other members of the group and
discuss the meaning of the poem.

a) Is the rhythm of the verse slow, delicate, stuttering,
   fast?
b) Note down words which describe the woman.
c) Why has the phrase '*He took/Her arm*' been split on
   to separate lines?
d) What are the feelings of the man at the end of the
   poem?
e) What type of relationship do you think exists between the man and the woman?

A writer will often use images to communicate what he
imagines to you more clearly. Refer back to C16: both James
Joyce and Patience Strong have used images – word pictures.
You may feel, however, that the falling snow in Joyce's
passage is 'symbolic'. A symbol is a sign which represents
something. An exclamation mark in a red triangle is a symbol
of danger, a crucifix is a symbol of religious faith. A poet
may also use symbols to represent feelings.

Both poems which follow are concerned with broken
relationships:

FORGOTTEN ANNIVERSARY

The faceless newsman
delivered his ever battery-flat news
attempting to catch attentive break-fasters
As he told
of strikes
rapes
wars
broken contracts
and so they sat unresponding
sipping tepid tea
avoiding the life-creased lines
on her cardboard grey face
he read the cornflakes packet
'Could you pass the stirring spoon?'
she asked
trespassing on the stillness

half ashamed of her intrusion
he obliged
and silence resettled among
the marmalade, the crockery
the silver napkin rings.
He had forgotten her complexion
once resembled the pale-porcelain
of his cup
believing happy-ever afters were safer
run on routine.
Sitting tightlipped in her territory
She stared hard at the paper
unseeing, faking diverted attention
waiting
the clock perceiving the scene
through glazed pendulumed eye
ticked passionless seconds
waiting
the Staffordshire dogs displaying disdain
remained motionless
waiting
and still he sat silent
deaf to his cue
unaware of the suppressed expectancy
and so the tea-stained
tear stained
tableclothed distance
between
remained in roseless requiem.

Louise Gower (aged seventeen)

THE BEAUTIFUL TOILET

Blue, blue is the grass about the river
And the willows have overfilled the close garden.
And within, the mistress, in the midmost of her youth,
White, white of face, hesitates, passing the door.
Slender, she puts forth a slender hand;

And she was a courtezan in the old days,
And she has married a sot,
Who now goes drunkenly out
And leaves her too much alone.

Ezra Pound (attributed to Mei Sheng, 140 BC)

C37

Discuss the meaning of both poems.

In Louise Gower's poem:

a) What is the purpose of the frequent references to objects on the table and in the room?

b) In what sense was the remark *'Could you pass the stirring spoon?'* a trespass *'on the stillness'*?

c) Which words or phrases are particularly descriptive?

In Ezra Pound's poem:

i) The girl has *'married a sot'*. Is there anything in her surroundings which symbolises her present life?

ii) What are the major differences between her married life and her previous life as a *'courtezan'*?

iii) The final line could have been written
   'And leaves her alone too much'
   Which way is more effective and why?

iv) Why are the words *'blue'* and *'white'* repeated?

C38

List the different methods used by each poet (type of language, description, shape, rhythm).

Rhythm and rhyme

C39

In C21 we mentioned sincerity and insincerity in prose. In criticising poetry, we are looking for writing which is relaxed and fluent; sometimes, however, we may meet writing that sounds 'forced' or 'artificial'.

In pop songs we sometimes hear some very painful rhyming lyrics. Most pop song lyrics would be very unlikely to 'stand up' as poetry. Write down the lyrics of a pop song and decide this for yourself.

The next three poems or poetic extracts all use rhyme and rhythm deliberately, but for different reasons.

The first two use lines which rhyme in pairs, known as rhyming couplets.

Just now the lilac is in bloom,
All before my little room;
And in my flower-beds, I think,
Smile the carnation and the pink;
And down the borders, well I know,
The poppy and the pansy blow . . . .
Oh! there the chestnuts, summer through,
Beside the river make for you
A tunnel of green gloom, and sleep
Deeply above; and green and deep
The stream mysterious glides beneath,
Green as a dream and deep as death.

Ah God! to see the branches stir
Across the moon at Grantchester!
To smell the thrilling – sweet and rotten,
Unforgettable, unforgotten
River smell, and hear the breeze
Sobbing in the little trees.

from THE OLD VICARAGE, GRANTCHESTER by Rupert Brooke

Beautiful new railway bridge of the Silvery Tay,
With your strong brick piers and buttresses in so grand array,
And your thirteen central girders, which seem to my eye
Strong enough all windy storms to defy.
And as I gaze upon thee my heart feels gay,
Because thou are the greatest railway bridge of the present day
And can be seen for miles away
From north, south, east or west of the Tay
On a beautiful clear and sunshiny day, . . .

from AN ADDRESS TO THE NEW TAY BRIDGE
by William McGonagall

Spike Milligan, however, uses these techniques for deliberately comic effect.

SOLDIER FREDDY

Soldier Freddy
*   was never ready,*
But! Soldier Neddy,
*   unlike Freddy*
*Was **always** ready*
*   and steady,*

That's why,
*   When Soldier Neddy*
Is-outside-Buckingham-Palace-on-guard-in-the-
*   pouring-wind-and-rain-*
*   being-steady-and-ready,*

Freddy –
*   is home in beddy.*

Spike Milligan

How successful are these poems? Do the first two help you to look at a woodland scene and a bridge in a fresh and original way? Look closely at some of the descriptive language and rhyming couplets used: do they add to the descriptive quality and language of the poems or detract from it?

Note down any words or expressions you do not like and attempt to give a reason.

SPRING

Nothing *is so beautiful as Spring –*
*   When weeds, in wheels, shoot long and lovely and lush;*
*   Thrush's eggs look little low heavens, and thrush*
Through the echoing timber does so rinse and wring
The ear, it strikes like lightnings to hear him sing:
*   The glassy peartree leaves and blooms, they brush*
*   The descending blue; that blue is all in a rush*
With richness; the racing lambs too have fair their fling.

What is all this juice and all this joy?
*   A strain of the earth's sweet being in the beginning*
In Eden garden. – Have, get, before it cloy,
*   Before it cloud, Christ, lord, and sour with sinning,*
Innocent mind and Mayday in girl and boy,
*   Most, O maid's child, thy choice and worthy the winning.*

Gerard Manley Hopkins

You will have already noticed a distinct difference in the techniques used in SPRING when compared to the verse already examined. There is an urgency, an intensity, a sense of compression in the poet's use of words.
Discuss the meaning of the poem, paying attention to any difficult expressions.

C40

Why are the ideas of spring, innocence and first love brought together at the end of the poem?

C41

Poets use the following techniques to add to the effectiveness of their descriptive writing:

a) Onomatopoeia: this involves the use of words whose sounds adds to their meaning; for example: '*echoing*' (line four).

When Batman and Robin finally tangle with 'The Joker' in Gotham City, a fight begins: Batman punches The Joker – **Zap!**; Joker punches Batman **Thrrokk!** Robin intervenes and punches Batman by mistake **Pow!** All these invented words are onomatopoeic because their sound or some quality in them implies their meaning. Other examples are **Bang** and **Crash**. Can you think of any more?

Write down onomatopoeic words to describe the following:

> a breeze, a pistol firing, cars colliding, a storm, a waterfall, a door closing.

b) Alliteration: this involves the use of two or more words in close succession which begin with the same consonant:

> *The fair breeze blew, the white floam flew;*
> *The furrow followed free.*

Hopkins uses this method in line two of his poem. Here the repeated strong 'l' sounds of *'long and lovely and lush'* add to the feeling of richness and fertility implied in the line.

Similarly, in lines six and seven the alliterative effect *'blooms'*, *'brush'* and *'blue'* adds to the impression of vivid splashes of colour.
Find some more examples.

c) Assonance: poets sometimes use a series of words which contain a similar vowel sound. Look at line five of SPRING. The repeated 'i' sound complements the 'echoing' effect of birdsong in the previous line.

Louise Gower also uses these effects in her poem FORGOTTEN ANNIVERSARY (C 36):

> *'Sitting tight lipped in her territory'.*

Both the use of assonance and the alliterative 't' sound add to the impression of confined restricted movement experienced by the wife.

C42

Finally in our consideration of verse, look at Wilfred Owen's war poem EXPOSURE in which he describes a tense silence in the battle. Notice the use of techniques already described, in addition to his varied but consistent use of rhythm.

EXPOSURE

Our brains ache, in the merciless iced east winds that knive
  us ...
Wearied we keep awake because the night is silent ...
Low, drooping flares confuse our memory of the salient ...

Worried by silence, sentries whisper, curious, nervous,
            But nothing happens.

Watching, we hear the mad gusts tugging on the wire,
Like twitching agonies of men among its brambles.
Northward, incessantly, the flickering gunnery rumbles,
Far off, like a dull rumour of some other war.
            What are we doing here?

The poignant misery of dawn begins to grow ...
We only know war lasts, rain soaks, and clouds sag stormy.
Dawn massing in the east her melancholy army
Attacks once more in ranks on shivering ranks of gray,
            But nothing happens.

Sudden successive flights of bullets streak the silence.
Less deathly than the air that shudders black with snow,
With sidelong flowing flakes that flock, pause and renew;
We watch them wandering up and down the wind's nonchalance,
            But nothing happens.

Pale flakes with fingering stealth come feeling for our faces —
We cringe in holes, back on forgotten dreams, and stare, snow-
      dazed,
Deep into grassier ditches. So we drowse, sun-dozed,
Littered with blossoms trickling where the blackbird fusses.
            Is it that we are dying?

Slowly our ghosts drag home: glimpsing the sunk fires, glozed
With crusted dark-red jewels; crickets jingle there;
For hours the innocent mice rejoice: the house is theirs;
Shutters and doors, all closed: on us the doors are closed —
            We turn back to our dying.

Since we believe not otherwise can kind fires burn;
Nor ever suns smile true on child, or field, or fruit.
For God's invincible spring our love is made afraid;
Therefore, not loath, we lie out here; therefore were born,
            For love of God seems dying.

Tonight, His frost will fasten on this mud and us,
Shrivelling many hands, puckering foreheads crisp.
The burying-party, picks and shovels in their shaking grasp,
Pause over half-known faces. All their eyes are ice,
            But nothing happens.

                                           Wilfred Owen

You may have noticed the technique of 'half-rhyme' here (different vowels sound in words which would otherwise rhyme exactly). What effect does this have on the tone of the poem?

Drama

Good dialogue is probably among the most difficult of written forms. Dialogue in drama must not only make good reading, but it must also convey the character of the speaker. It must be appropriate to the character: an archbishop would be unlikely to say 'Bless yer, my old son!' although it's an amusing thought.

It must also be lively and entertaining and not contain trivia:

> SHARON: (*Rings doorbell. Ring-ring.*) Hello Debbie.
> DEBBIE: Hello Sharon.
> SHARON: How are you?
> DEBBIE: Fine. How are you?
> SHARON: Fine.
> DEBBIE: You coming up the club then?
> SHARON: Yeh. All right.

It is very unlikely that you will have heard anything like this in the theatre, on television or at the cinema. We can assume that Sharon and Debbie know each other; therefore the play should really start as they enter the club.

Trivial dialogue is often called stereotyped. Drama that is overworked or exaggerated to a ludicrous extent is called melodrama. In this extract, Tom Stoppard is using stereotyped language and melodramatic emotion deliberately:

> *Scene: Muldoon Manor; the lounge. Cynthia enters and sees Simon.*
>
> CYNTHIA: Simon!
> SIMON: Cynthia!
> CYNTHIA: Don't say anything for a moment – just hold me.
> (*He seizes her and glues his lips to hers, as they say. Cynthia breaks dramatically away.*)

CYNTHIA: We can't go on meeting like this!
SIMON: We have nothing to be ashamed of!
CYNTHIA: But darling, this is madness!
SIMON: Yes! I am mad with love for you!
CYNTHIA: Please! Remember where we are!
SIMON: Cynthia, I love you!
CYNTHIA: Don't – I love Albert!
SIMON: He's dead! (*Shaking her*) Do you understand me – Albert's dead!
CYNTHIA: No – I'll never give up hope! Let me go! We are not free!
SIMON: I don't care, we were meant for each other – had we but met in time.
CYNTHIA: You're a cad, Simon! You will use me and cast me aside as you have cast aside so many others.
SIMON: No, Cynthia! – you can make me a better person!
CYNTHIA: You're ruthless – so strong, so cruel – (*Ruthlessly he kisses her. Cynthia breaks away.*)
CYNTHIA: Stop – can't you see you're making a fool of yourself!
SIMON: I'll kill anyone who comes between us!

from THE REAL INSPECTOR HOUND by Tom Stoppard

Perform this short scene:

a)   as comedy
b)   as serious theatre.

Introduce a third character, for example, a male or female rival, Cynthia's father, or even 'Albert' returning unexpectedly as a ghost or in disguise!

Can you develop the scene into a 'whodunnit'? Outline your plot and discuss characters with a partner or small group.

The love story of ROMEO AND JULIET by William Shakespeare is world-famous and has been the subject of many modern adaptations. In this scene, Romeo encounters Juliet as she looks from the window of her father's house into the orchard. You may remember that the two lovers come from families who are sworn enemies, the Capulets and the Montagues.

JULIET: O Romeo, Romeo! wherefore art thou Romeo?
   Deny thy father and refuse thy name;
   Or, if thou wilt not, be but sworn my love,   35
   And I'll no longer be a Capulet.
ROMEO: [*Aside*] Shall I hear more, or shall I speak at this?
JULIET: 'T is but thy name that is my enemy;
   Thou art thyself, though not a Montague.
   What's Montague? it is nor hand, nor foot,
   Nor arm, nor face, nor any other part
   Belonging to a man. O, be some other name!
   What's in a name? that which we call a rose
   By any other name would smell as sweet;
   So Romeo would, were he not Romeo call'd,
   Retain that dear perfection which he owes
   Without that title. Romeo, doff thy name,
   And for that name which is no part of thee
   Take all myself.
ROMEO: I take thee at thy word:
   Call me but love, and I'll be new baptised;   50
   Henceforth I never will be Romeo.
JULIET: What man art thou that thus bescreen'd in night
   So stumblest on my counsel?
ROMEO: By a name
   I know not how to tell thee who I am:
   My name, dear saint, is hateful to myself,   55
   Because it is an enemy to thee;
   Had I it written, I would tear the word.
JULIET: My ears have not yet drunk a hundred words
   Of that tongue's utterance, yet I know the sound:
   Art thou not Romeo and a Montague?   60
ROMEO: Neither, fair saint, if either thee dislike.
JULIET: How cam'st thou hither, tell me, and wherefore?
   The orchard walls are high and hard to climb,
   And the place death, considering who thou art,
   If any of my kinsmen find thee here.   65
ROMEO: With love's light wings did I o'er-perch these
        walls;
   For stony limits cannot hold love out,
   And what love can do that dares love attempt;
   Therefore thy kinsmen are no let to me.
JULIET: If they do see thee, they will murder thee.   70
ROMEO: Alack, there lies more peril in thine eye
   Than twenty of their swords: look thou but sweet,
   And I am proof against their enmity.

JULIET: I would not for the world they saw thee here.
ROMEO: I have night's cloak to hide me from their sight,
   And but thou love me, let them find me here: 75
   My life were better ended by their hate,
   Than death prorogued, wanting of thy love.
JULIET: By whose direction found'st thou out this place?
ROMEO: By love, who first did prompt me to inquire;   80
   He lent me counsel and I lent him eyes.
   I am no pilot; yet, wert thou as far
   As that vast shore wash'd with the farthest sea,
   I would adventure for such merchandise.
JULIET: Thou know'st the mask of night is on my face,   85
   Else would a maiden blush bepaint my cheek
   For that which thou hast heard me speak to-night.
   Fain would I dwell on form, fain, fain deny
   What I have spoke: but farewell compliment!
   Dost thou love me? I know thou wilt say 'Ay,'   90
   And I will take thy word: yet, if thous swear'st,
   Thou mayst prove false; at lovers' perjuries,
   They say, Jove laughs. O gentle Romeo,
   If thou dost love, pronounce it faithfully:
   Or if thou think'st I am too quickly won,   95
   I'll frown and be perverse and say thee nay,
   So thou wilt woo; but else, not for the world.
   In truth, fair Montague, I am too fond,
   And therefore thou mayst think my 'haviour light:
   But trust me, gentleman, I'll prove more true   100
   Than those that have more cunning to be strange.
   I should have been more strange, I must confess,
   But that thou overheard'st, ere I was ware,
   My true love's passion: therefore pardon me,
   And not impute this yielding to light love,   105
   Which the dark night hath so discovered.
ROMEO: Lady, by yonder blessed moon I swear
   That tips with silver all these fruit-tree tops –
JULIET: O, swear not by the moon, the inconstant moon,
   That monthly changes in her circled orb,   110
   Lest that thy love prove likewise variable.
ROMEO: What shall I swear by?
JULIET: Do not swear at all;
   Or, if thou wilt, swear by thy gracious self,
   Which is the god of my idolatry,
   And I'll believe thee.

a) Trace the development of Juliet's feelings during the scene.
b) Some of the speeches contain images which are references to objects and colours. How appropriate are they to this love scene?
c) Why are there so many references to light and dark in the speeches?
d) Are there any qualities in the language which are unfamiliar to you?

As with any of the drama passages in this section, greater understanding can be gained from acting this scene and, indeed, improvising a modern version based on a similar situation.

C48

One modern version of the Romeo and Juliet story is the musical WEST SIDE STORY. The rival families are now two New York street gangs, the Jets and the Sharks. They have decided to settle their differences with a fight and the Jets, featured in this scene and led by Riff, meet at Doc's drugstore for a war council with the Sharks.

Midnight. The drugstore.

A suggestion of a run-down, musty general store which in cities, is called a drugstore. A door leading to the street outside; another leading to the cellar below.

Baby John is reading a comic book; A-rab is playing solitaire; Anybodys is huddled by the juke box; Action is watching the street door. The atmosphere is tense, jumpy. Action slams the door and strides to the dart board.

ACTION: Where the devil are they? Are we havin' a war council to-night or ain't we?

(*He throws a dart savagely.*)

BABY JOHN: He don't use knives. He don't even use an atomic ray gun.
A-RAB: Who don't?
BABY JOHN: Superman. Gee, I love him.
SNOWBOY: So marry him.
ANYBODYS: I ain't never gonna get married: too noisy.
A-RAB: You ain't never gonna get married: too ugly.

ANYBODYS ('*Shooting*' *him*):   Pow pow!

A-RAB: Cracko, jacko! (*Clutching his belly, he spins to the floor*) Down goes a teen-age hoodlum.

BABY JOHN: Could a zip gun make you do like that?

(*A second of silence. Then Snowboy slams into the room and they all jump.*)

ACTION: What the hell's a matter with you?

SNOWBOY: I got caught sneakin' outa the movies.

A-RAB: Sneakin' **out?** Wadd'ya do that for?

SNOWBOY: I sneaked in.

ACTION: A war council comin' up and he goes to the movies.

ANYBODYS: And you let him be a Jet!

BABY JOHN: Ah, go walk the streets like ya sister.

ANYBODYS (*Jumping him*):   Lissen, jail bait, I licked you twice and I can do it again.

(*From the doorway behind the counter a little middle-aged man enters: Doc.*)

DOC: Curfew, gentlemen. And lady. Baby John, you should be home in bed.

BABY JOHN: We're gonna have a war council here, Doc.

DOC: A who?

A-RAB: To decide on weapons for a big-time rumble!

SNOWBOY: We're gonna mix with the PRs.

DOC: Weapons? You couldn't play basketball.

ANYBODYS: Get with it, buddy boy.

DOC: War councils –

ACTION: Don't start, Doc.

DOC: Rumbles . . .

ACTION: Doc –

DOC: Why, when I was your age –

ACTION: When you was my age; when my old man was my age; when my brother was my age! **You was never my age, none a you!** The sooner you creeps get hip to that, the sooner you'll dig us.

DOC: I'll dig your early graves, that's what I'll dig.

A-RAB: Dig, dig, dig –

DOC: What're you gonna be when you grow up?

ANYBODYS (*Wistfully*):   A telephone call girl!

(*The store doorbell tinkles as Riff enters with Velma.*)

SNOWBOY: Riff, hey!

ACTION: Are they comin'?

RIFF: Unwind, Action. Hey, Doc, Tony here?

DOC: No, Riff, it's closing time.

ACTION (To Riff):   What d'ya think they're gonna ask for?

A-RAB: Just rubber hoses, maybe, huh?

RIFF: Cool, little men. Easy, freezy cool.

VELMA: Oo, oo, ooblee – oo.

(*Diesel enters with a would-be grand number: Graziella.*)

DIESEL: They're comin' any minute now!

ACTION: Chung chung!

A-RAB: Cracko, jacko!

VELMA: Ooblee-oo.

RIFF (Sharply):   Cool!

ANYBODYS: Riff – in a tight spot you need every man you can –

RIFF: No.

GRAZIELLA (Indicating Anybodys to Velma):   An American tragedy.

ANYBODYS ('Shooting' her):   Pow.

GRAZIELLA: Poo.

VELMA: Ooblee-pooh.

(*They giggle.*)

RIFF: Now when the victims come in, you chicks cut out.

GRAZIELLA: We might, and then again we might not.

DIESEL: This ain't kid stuff, Graziella.

GRAZIELLA: I and Velma ain't kid stuff, neither. Are we, Vel?

VELMA: No thank you-oo, ooblee-oo.

GRAZIELLA: And you can punctuate it?

VELMA: Ooo!

(*They giggle again.*)

ACTION (To Riff):   What're we poopin' around with dumb broads?

GRAZIELLA: I and Velma ain't dumb!

ACTION: We got important business comin'.

DOC: Makin' trouble for the Puerto Ricans?

SNOWBOY: They make trouble for us.

DOC: Look! He almost laughs when he says it. For you, trouble is a relief.

RIFF: We've got to stand up to the PRs, Doc. It's important.

DOC: Fighting over a little piece of street is so important?

ACTION: To us, it is.

DOC: To hoodlums, it is.

(*He goes out through the cellar doorway as Action lunges for him.*)

ACTION: Don't you call me hoodlum!

RIFF (*Holding him*): Easy, Action! Save your steam for the rumble.

A-RAB: He don't want what we want, so we're hoodlums!

BABY JOHN: I wear a jacket like my buddies, so my teacher calls me hoodlum!

ACTION: I swear the next creep who calls me hoodlum –

RIFF: **You'll laugh!** Yeah. Now you all better dig this and dig it the most. No matter who or what is eatin' at you, you show it, buddy boys, and **you are dead**. You are cuttin' a hole in yourselves for them to stick in a red hot umbrella and open it. Wide. You wanna live? You play it cool.

(*Music starts.*)

ACTION: I wanna get even!
RIFF: Get cool.
A-RAB: I wanna bust!
RIFF: Bust cool.
BABY JOHN: I wanna go!
RIFF: **Go cool!**

Deciding on how to perform this scene demands a clear impression of each character. Do the lines immediately show how they are meant to be spoken? Can you visualise the character of Doc clearly? Is the pace and rhythm of his lines appropriate to the way he would speak?

There are phrases in the passage which have become clichés. Do they still work?

C49

The following speech is from Harold Pinter's play THE CARETAKER. Aston is one of two brothers who befriends a tramp, Davies. Aston behaves strangely throughout the play: in this extract he is explaining his supposed 'mental illness' to Davies. He has just mentioned a cafe that he used to go to:

Spent quite a bit of time in there. That was before I went away. Just before. I think that – place had a lot to do with it. They were all – a good bit older than me. But they always used to listen. I thought – they understood what I said. I mean I used to talk to them. I talked too much. That was my mistake. The same in the factory. Standing there, or in the breaks, I used to – talk about things, and these men they used to listen, whenever I – had anything to say. It was all right. (*He stops sandpapering*) The trouble was, I used to have kind of hallucinations. They weren't hallucinations, they – I used to get the feeling I could see things – very clearly – everything – was so clear – everything used – everything used to get very quiet – everything got very quiet – all this – quiet – and this clear sight – it was – but maybe I was wrong. Anyway, someone must have said something. I didn't know anything about it. And – some kind of lie must have got around. And this lie went round. I thought people started being funny. In that café. The factory. I couldn't understand it. Then one day they took me to a hospital, right outside London. They – got me there. I didn't want to go. Anyway – I tried to get out, quite a few times. But – it wasn't very easy. They asked me questions, in there. Got me in and asked me all sorts of questions. Well, I told them – when they wanted to know – what my thoughts were. Hmmnn. Then one day – this man – doctor, I suppose – the head one – he was quite a man of – distinction – although I wasn't so sure about that. He called me in. He said – he told me I had something. He said they'd concluded their examination. That's what he said. And he showed me a pile of papers and he said that I'd got something, some complaint. He said – he just said that, you see. You've got – this thing. That's your complaint. And we've decided, he said, that in your interests there's only one course we can take – he said, we're going to do something to your brain. He said – if we don't, you'll be in here for the rest of your life, but if we do, you stand a chance. You can go out, he said, and live like the others. What do you want to do to my brain, I said to him. But he just repeated what he'd said. Well, I wasn't a fool. I knew I was a minor. I knew he couldn't do anything to me without getting permission. I knew he had to get permission from my mother. So I wrote to her and told her what they were trying to do. But she signed their form, you see, giving them permission. I know that because he showed me her signature when I brought it up. Well, that night I tried to escape, that night. I spent five hours sawing at one of the bars on the window of this ward. Right throughout the dark. They used to shine a torch over the beds every half hour. So I timed it just right. And then it was nearly done, and a man had a – he had a fit, right next to me. And they caught me, anyway. About a week later they started to come round and do this thing to the brain. We were all supposed to have it done, in this ward. And they came round and did it one at a time. One a night. I was one of the last. And I could see quite clearly what they did to the others. They used to come round with these – I don't know what they were – they looked like big pincers, with wires on, the wires were attached to a little machine. It was electric. They used to hold the man down, and this chief – the chief doctor, used to fit the pincers, something like earphones, he used to fit them on either side of the man's skull. There was a man holding the machine, you see, and he'd turn it on, and the chief would just press

these pincers on either side of the skull and keep them there.
Then he'd take them off. They'd cover the man up – and
they wouldn't touch him again until later on. Some used
to put up a fight, but most of them didn't. They just lay
there. Well, they were coming round to me, and the night
they came I got up and stood against the wall. They told
me to get on the bed, and I knew they had to get me on
the bed because if they did it while I was standing up they
might break my spine. So I stood up and then one or two
of them came for me, well, I was younger then, I was much
stronger than I am now, I was quite strong then, I laid one
of them out and I had another one round the throat, and
then suddenly this chief had these pincers on my skull and
I knew he wasn't supposed to do it while I was standing
up that's why I ... anyway, he did it. So I did get out.
I got out of the place – but I couldn't walk very well. I
don't think my spine was damaged. That was perfectly all
right. The trouble was – my thoughts – had become very
slow – I couldn't think at all – I couldn't – get – my
thoughts – together – uuuhh – I could – never quite get
it – together. The trouble was, I couldn't hear what people
were saying. I couldn't look to the right or the left, I had
to look straight in front of me, because if I turned my head
round – I couldn't keep – upright. And I had these head-
aches. I used to sit in my room. That was when I lived with
my mother. And my brother. He was younger than me.
And I laid everything out, in order, in my room, all the
things I knew were mine, but I didn't die. The thing is,
I should have been dead. I should have died. Anyway, I
feel much better now. But I don't talk to people now. I
steer clear of places like that café. I never go into them now.
I don't talk to anyone – like that. I've often thought of going
back and trying to find the man who did that to me. But
I want to do something first. I want to build that shed out
in the garden.

CURTAIN

What impression do you get of Aston from this speech? How
does it reveal his character?

Work through the speech carefully, deciding how to deal
with the hesitations and changing lines of thought.

How would Aston be acting, behaving, as he speaks?

Index by theme

Acknowledgements

The authors and publishers wish to thank the following for their permission to reproduce printed matter:

page 4, Ted Hughes, 'Horses' from *The Hawk in the Rain* (Faber and Faber Ltd); page 10, The Trustees for the copyrights of the late Dylan Thomas, from *A Portrait of the Artist as a Young Dog* (J. M. Dent & Sons); pages 11, 16 and 37, Laurie Lee, from *As I Walked Out One Midsummer Morning* (1969 edition, Andre Deutsch Ltd); page 13, William Golding, from *Lord of the Flies* (Faber and Faber Ltd); page 14, Norman Nicholson, 'Belshazzar' from *Five Rivers* (Faber and Faber Ltd); page 17, Jack Shaefer, from *Shane* (Andre Deutsch Ltd); page 20, Keith Waterhouse, from *Billy Liar* (Michael Joseph Ltd); page 22, Alan Garner, from *Red Shift* (William Collins Sons & Co Ltd); page 25, Frederick Forsyth, from *The Day of the Jackal* (Hutchinson Publishing Group Ltd); page 33, James Joyce, from *Ulysses* (The Bodley Head); page 33, Demetrios Capetanakis, 'Detective Story' (John Lemann); page 34, W. H. Auden, 'O What is that Sound' from *Collected Shorter Poems* (Faber and Faber Ltd); pages 37 and 116, The Executors of the Ernest Hemingway Estate, from *A Farewell to Arms* and 'The End of Something' from *The First Forty-nine Stories* (Jonathan Cape Ltd); page 40, 'Jacks not all right' (The Observer, 25 February 1979); page 42, 'United Sweep to their Title' (The Observer, 7 May 1967); page 44, John Prebble, from *Culloden* (Martin Secker and Warburg Ltd); page 51, Louis MacNeice, 'For X' from *The Collected Poems of Louis MacNeice* (Faber and Faber Ltd); page 52, Desmond Morris, from *Manwatching* (Jonathan Cape Ltd); pages 55–8, Vance Packard, from *The Hidden Persuaders* and *The Status Seekers* (by permission of A. P. Watt Ltd); page 59, Fitline Jump Rope Company; page 64, Peter Terson, from *Zigger Zagger/Mooney and his Caravans* (Penguin Books Ltd); page 72, Charles Lyte, 'If you Want to Get Ahead, Get Smart' (The Daily Mirror, 16 September 1977); page 79, Alan Bullock, from *Hitler: A Study in Tyranny* (Hamlyn Group Ltd); page 82, William Shirer, from *The Rise and Fall of the Third Reich* (Martin Secker and Warburg Ltd); page 86, Roger McGough, 'Why Patriots are a bit Nuts in the Head' (© 1967 by Roger McGough, from Penguin Modern Poets Volume 10); page 87, George Orwell, from *The Sporting Spirit* (Tribune, 1945); page 88, Harvey Andrews, 'Hello Hans' (Essex Music International Ltd); page 90, D. H. Lawrence, from 'Pornography and Obscenity' from *Phoenix* and from 'Introduction to 'Pansies'' from *The Complete Poems of D. H. Lawrence* (William Heinemann Ltd; acknowledgement is also made to Lawrence Pollinger Ltd and the Estate of the late Mrs Frieda Lawrence Ravagli); page 90, Max Caulfield, from *Mary Whitehouse* (A. R. Mowbray & Co Ltd); page 91, George Orwell, from *Nineteen Eighty Four* (Martin Secker and Warburg Ltd; acknowledgement is also made to Mrs Sonia Brownell Orwell); page 92, Notice on Censorship (Greater London Council); page 97, 'Carburetter cold start adjustment' (Vauxhall Motors Ltd); page 100, Rowland Hilder, 'Starting with Watercolours' (Cassell Ltd); page 106, Hugh Montefiore, from *Taking our Past into our Future* (William Collins Sons & Co Ltd); page 107, 'Air France Sees Concorde Loss' (New York Times, 13 December 1978); page 108, 'Concorde Damage: Commission Meets Friday' (L'Orient-le Jour, Beirut 12 May

1979); pages 108 and 110, 'Latest Concorde Costs' and 'Concorde USA: Decision Awaited' (Flight International, 10 April 1979 and 17 January 1976); page 108, 'Concorde in £17 Dogfight' (Daily Star, 20 March 1979); page 109, 'The High Life. Can You afford *not* to fly Concorde?' (British Airways); page 113, Patience Strong, 'Winter Fantasy' (Woman's Own, 12 February 1979); page 113, The Executors of the James Joyce Estate, from *The Dead* (Jonathan Cape Ltd); page 115, Audrie Manley-Tucker, from *This Year is for Me* (Woman & Home, February 1979); page 135, Ezra Pound, 'The Beautiful Toilet' from *Collected Shorter Poems* (Faber and Faber Ltd); page 137, William McGonagall, from *An Address to the New Tay Bridge* (Gerald Duckworth & Co Ltd); page 137, Spike Milligan, 'Soldier Freddy' from *A Dustbin of Milligan* (Dennis Dobson Books Ltd); page 141, Wilfred Owen, 'Exposure' from *The Collected Poems of Wilfred Owen* (Edited by C. Day Lewis. Acknowledgement is made to The Owen Estate and Chatto and Windus Ltd): page 142, Tom Stoppard, from *The Real Inspector Hound* (Faber and Faber Ltd); page 146, Laurents and Sondheim, from *West Side Story* (© 1972 by Arthur Laurents, from Heinemann Educational Ltd); page 150, Harold Pinter, from Act 3 of *The Caretaker* (Eyre Methuen Ltd).

The authors and publishers also wish to thank the following for permission to reproduce illustrations:

page 3, Derek Widdicombe; page 4, The Tate Gallery; pages 5, 21, 114, 139, Popperfoto; pages 11, 12 (two photographs), 18, 53, Nick Thomas; pages 19, 93, ILEA 'Contact' (Inner London Education Authority Teacher's Magazine); page 23, Manchester City Art Gallery; page 29, courtesy of National Film Archive/Stills Library; pages 35, 36 (three photographs), 75, Alan Hayward, Senior Lecturer in Communications and Learning Resources, King Alfred's College, Winchester; pages 39, 65, Keystone Press Agency; pages 46, 81, 85, 86, the Imperial War Museum; page 59, Arthur Guinness Son & Co Ltd; page 60 (top), Cadbury Ltd; page 60 (bottom), John Harvey & Sons Ltd; page 61, Anne French Ltd; page 70, Crown copyright, Manpower Services Commission; page 72 (two photographs), Syndication International Ltd; page 83, Press Association; page 102, Pablo Picasso, 'Guernica', 1937, oil on canvas, $11'5\frac{1}{2}''$ by $25'5\frac{3}{4}''$ – Collection, The Museum of Modern Art, New York, on loan from the artist's estate; pages 105, 109 (two photographs), British Airways; pages 111, 130, © British Museum; page 114, Walker Art Gallery; page 123, Brian Long; front cover, 'Tiger by a Stream' by Kishi Ganku, British Museum; back cover, 'Still Life with Fruit' by Jan van Streek, Ashmolean Museum.

The publishers have made every effort to trace copyright-holders, but if they have inadvertently overlooked any they will be pleased to make the necessary arrangements at the first opportunity.